DATE DUE

NOV

MA
NO

N

SUICIDE

CLINICAL AND EPIDEMIOLOGICAL STUDIES

Brian Barraclough
Senior Lecturer in Psychiatry,
Faculty of Medicine,
University of Southampton

with

Jennifer Hughes
Senior Research Fellow in Psychiatry,
Faculty of Medicine,
University of Southampton.

CROOM HELM
London • New York • Sydney

© 1987 Brian Barraclough
Croom Helm Ltd, Provident House,
Burrell Row, Beckenham, Kent BR3 1AT
Croom Helm Australia, 44–50 Waterloo Road,
North Ryde, 2113, New South Wales

Published in the USA by
Croom Helm
in association with Methuen, Inc.
29 West 35th Street
New York, NY 10001

British Library Cataloguing in Publication Data

Barraclough, Brian M.
   Suicide: clinical and epidemiological
   studies.
   1. Suicide
   I. Title   II. Hughes, Jennifer
   616.85'8445   RC569

   ISBN 0–7099–5009–8

Library of Congress Cataloging in Publication Data
ISBN 0–7099–5009–8

Printed and bound in Great Britain
by Billings & Sons Limited, Worcester.

Contents

Introduction

Suicide accounts for about 4,000 deaths every year in England and Wales: about 1 per cent of deaths for all age groups combined. For young adults the proportion of deaths from this cause is much higher: 7 per cent of deaths among those aged 15–24 are from suicide. Suicide is exceeded only by accidents and cancers in numerical importance as a cause of death in younger age groups. The large number of premature deaths which result from suicide often give rise to widowing, orphaning and economic loss. Those bereaved as a result of suicide often have to face social and financial problems of a particularly gruelling kind. The prevention of suicide is therefore an important medical and social challenge.

Prevention of suicide is not always considered desirable. Suicide is sometimes viewed as a brave and noble act, the free choice of a free man in a philosophical crisis. These romantic views are sustained by the idealisation of suicide often found in literature and on the stage. Such concepts of suicide bear scant relationship to suicide in real life, which so often takes place in sordid circumstances as the culmination of prolonged, intractable mental illness and disordered social lives. Other opponents of suicide prevention, more pragmatic in their approach, argue that the suicide of the incurably physically or mentally ill should not be obstructed, or even that it should be encouraged. This argument is sound for those cases in which every avenue of treatment has been thoroughly pursued, and if there is no hope of eventual recovery. Few cases of suicide meet these criteria.

Suicide is unique to man. The definition of suicide — conscious behaviour which is intended to result in self-murder — requires an ability to conceptualise death which is not possessed by other living creatures. Some animals in their natural habitat do behave in a way which results in their own immediate death: whales and lemmings for instance among mammals, and some social insects. Primates kept in stressful captivity have been seen to mutilate themselves fatally, but death does not seem to have been their intention.

Theories and speculation about suicide abound, whereas factual knowledge of the subject which is based on sound

1

scientific inquiry is rather modest. The two theories about the causes of suicide with which this book is most concerned are the social theory associated, although not originating, with Durkheim, and the mental illness theory based on medical observation. They are to some extent theories in conflict.

Durkheim published *Le Suicide* in 1897 at the peak of his powers. His book brings together in an original way pre-existing ideas about the social origins of the rising suicide rates of the urban population during the European industrial revolution. The work is an interpretation of mid- and late nineteenth-century suicide and other vital statistics. Durkheim used these data to support his argument that suicide results from social causes which, at some risk of oversimplification, can be grouped into three types: altruistic, egoistic and anomic.

Altruistic suicide, exemplified in European eyes today by the suicide of Captain Oates and by ritual suicides in Oriental societies, is motivated by a wish to benefit others, free them of a burden, or comply with powerful social obligations. Egoistic suicide is the result of an individual having cut all ties with others as a consequence of his own conduct. The isolation which sometimes results from mental illness is an example. The term anomic suicide applies when the individual is isolated from others, not by his own choice or actions as in egoistic suicide, but by the structure of a society which prevents the maintenance of meaningful bonds between individuals. The unstable populations found in most large city centres, and the rapid readjustment required by populations experiencing industrialisation, political upheaval or mass migration, are examples. Egoistic and anomic suicide to some extent coexist, the inside and outside of the same glove.

Durkheim's theory, attractive because it explains so much, has had a great influence on the development of subsequent thinking about the causes of suicide. But his theory is not scientific in the sense that Popper uses the word, for it is not based on an hypothesis amenable to refutation. However, his theories do generate testable hypotheses and are valuable because of that. Durkheim placed little emphasis on the symptoms, social effects and social causes of mental illness as precursors of suicide. Knowing little medicine may be the reason, but his ambition to advance his subject, sociology, possibly contributed to a somewhat one-sided view.

The mental illness theory has fewer adherents than Durkheim's, especially in non-medical circles, but has the greater antiquity, being at the root of the coroner's rider 'suicide while the balance of the mind was disturbed', and its precursors. These devices mitigated the penalties inflicted on the body and the estate of the suicide believed to result from self-murder while rational. According to this theory, both now and in the past, suicide results from symptoms such as intense despair and hopelessness, unjustified guilt and self-deprecation, delusions of suicide, instructions of hallucinatory voices, or other intolerable mental experiences. Such symptoms probably originate in biological disturbances affecting brain function.

Severe illnesses of this kind are often followed and sometimes preceded by social breakdown in the person's life, disruption of family, loss of friendship, loss of work and its sequelae. In this way mental illness accounts at least in part for the correlations between the suicide rate and the social measurements which Durkheim and his followers have used to support social explanations of suicide.

There is much evidence in support of both theories for the countries of the West, although not for the remainder of the world apart from a few modernised Asian states. Clearly one theory cannot be correct to the exclusion of the other, and so the scientific task ahead is the integration of both theories — in my view a soluble problem requiring rather more than the under-funded and somewhat underpowered efforts of the recent past.

The methods available for studying suicide are largely retrospective ones, which entail interpreting statistics, and collecting observations recalled or recorded about the speech and conduct of those who die by suicide. The recent developments in laboratory skill, which permit a study of the brain bio-chemistry of the dead, have not yet produced consistent results.

Suicide mortality statistics are provided in all well-ordered countries of the world as part of the vital statistics service, often with legal overtones as in England. In many countries these statistics go back more than a century, providing a remarkable source of continuous data about trends in the incidence of suicide among various social groups. They record date, age, sex, marital status, and occupation for each death, and often the precise cause — for example poisoning, hanging, drowning. There are no comparable statistics for any other condition so closely linked to psychiatry; and no other cause of death, with the exception of homicide, for which such accurate continuous

3

statistics are available, since developments in modern medicine mean there is little continuity between today's diagnoses and those used 50 or 100 years ago.

Studies based upon large-scale statistics are most useful for testing social hypotheses about suicide. For research on the medical aspects, case studies are required, and these must by definition be retrospective. The record of the medicolegal inquiry, in England the inquest, has proved a useful source of data, but more relevant information can be gathered by medical and social scientists interviewing relatives and friends of the deceased soon after the death has taken place. A variation of the retrospective inquiry, the follow-up or follow-back of special groups studied in the past for purposes other than suicide research, has the advantage that the data were recorded during life, and are free of the bias likely to arise when witnesses recall the behaviour of a person who has since died.

Both statistical and case-study approaches have been used for the inquiries described in this book, which I conducted between 1965 and 1979 when employed by the Medical Research Council at its Clinical Psychiatry Unit in Graylingwell Hospital, Chichester, West Sussex.

Peter Sainsbury, the director of the unit, had carried out an inquiry into suicide in London (Sainsbury, 1955) to test hypotheses developed from Durkheim's social theory. He used a combined epidemiological and case-study approach, derived from the one so successfully employed by Faris and Dunham in their inquiry into the distribution of psychoses in Chicago (Faris and Dunham, 1939). Peter Sainsbury, the director of the unit, had carried out an inquiry into suicide in London to test hypotheses developed from Durkheim's social theory (Sainsbury 1955). He used a combined epidemiological and case study approach, derived from that employed so successfully by Faris and Dunham for their inquiry into the distribution of psychoses in Chicago (Faris and Dunham 1939). Sainsbury exploited the results of a social survey of London, combining the findings with data from a large number of London coroners' inquest notes. His interest in this approach had been stimulated by Sir Aubrey Lewis, Professor of Psychiatry at the Institute of Psychiatry, University of London, who had drawn Sainsbury's attention to these authors.

While reading the coroners' inquest notes, Sainsbury observed a high prevalence of both mental and physical ill-health, but especially mental ill-health, among those who committed suicide. He concluded that if treatable disease was a frequent precursor of suicide then it should be possible to prevent suicide by medical means. Such a view was contrary to Durkheim's strongly stated opinion, and to prevailing contemporary medical opinion as well.

The prevention of suicide is the strongest justification for inquiries into the topic. My recruitment to Sainsbury's unit provided an opportunity for a clinical study of suicide to investigate the evidence for a medical approach to prevention further than Sainsbury had been able to take it. Two studies in the United States of America (Robins, Murphy, Wilkinson *et al.*, 1959; Dorpat and Ripley, 1960) had claimed over 90 per cent of the suicides they had looked into were mentally ill. With two colleagues trained in psychiatric social work and clinical research methods I carried out an inquiry into the health and social circumstances of 100 consecutive suicides by interviewing relatives, and other informants, shortly after the death. This clinical inquiry, sometimes called a psychological autopsy in the United States of America, is the foundation of my knowledge about suicide. Interviewing relatives and collating the findings with information from other sources, written and verbal, brought me into as direct contact with the act of suicide, and what led up to it, as it is possible to be.

This inquiry led on to others, in the unplanned and untidy way that science develops, depending in my case on ideas and collaborators.

Some 5 years after the completion of the clinical inquiry we revisited the surviving spouses to describe the consequences of suicide for widows and children, not previously undertaken systematically. The results led us to question the prevailing view that survivors of suicide are bound to have a gloomy outlook, and to propose practical measures of support for those bereaved by suicide.

Criticism of the accuracy of official suicide statistics, much of it destructive and sometimes going so far as to dismiss statistics as useless, became frequent during the 1960s. The criticisms were difficult to refute, and hampered acceptance of our work. Papers on the accuracy of the suicide rate resulted from the spur of these criticisms.

Investigating the error of the suicide rate directed attention to self-inflicted deaths given open or accidental death verdicts.

Many are believed to be cases of suicide without enough evidence for a suicide verdict. These deaths had not been systematically studied before. Our inquiry set out to describe the similarities and differences between suicide and these other classes of self-inflicted death.

I became interested in the Samaritan organisation because of their bold claims to be able to prevent suicide. From my first-hand knowledge of the scope of illness and social disorder which precedes suicide, often for years, I thought that amateur counselling, no matter how well-intentioned, was unlikely to prevent the act, even if potential suicides were to seek out the Samaritans. Studies on the efficacy of suicide prevention by lay organisations were the result of this interest.

Acknowledgements

I would like to thank my collaborators over many years: Barbara Nelson and Jane Bunch (Mrs J.L. Gibbons), research psychiatric social workers, partners in the clinical inquiry; Marian Shea, a Samaritan worker who assisted with the inquiries about Samaritan clients; Daphne Shepherd, an academic psychiatric social worker whose interest led to the investigation of the aftermath of suicide for spouses and children; Trevor Holding, a registrar at Graylingwell Hospital and subsequently a Medical Research Council scientist, who carried out the inquest-based study of undetermined and accidental deaths: Christopher Jennings, my research assistant, and Jane Moss, who together worked out the difficult method for the controlled inquiry about Samaritan effectiveness; Ray Chynoweth, whose inquiry into suicides in Brisbane provided material for the clinical study on suicide and epilepsy; and Peter Fayers, who provided common-sense statistical advice over many years.

Coroners cannot be called collaborators. The friendly co-operation of Her Majesty's Coroners for West Sussex (F.F. Haddock and G.L.F. Bridgman) and for Portsmouth (P.D. Childs) advanced the clinical inquiry. The study of accidental and undetermined deaths was based on the inquest notes of Her Majesty's Coroner for Inner West London (G.L. Thurston).

To Peter Sainsbury I owe much for introducing me to a fascinating subject.

1

Mental Illness and Suicide

The suicide of an individual has traditionally been viewed, even in medical circles, as a moral or philosophical matter, rather than the potentially avoidable consequence of personal illness or unsatisfactory circumstances. The study of 100 suicides described here (Barraclough, Bunch, Nelson and Sainsbury, 1974) was designed to obtain information about the mental and physical health and social circumstances of an unselected sample of people who had committed suicide, with the intention of identifying practical strategies for suicide prevention, and of advancing knowledge about the subject of suicide in both its medical and social aspects.

Much evidence for the importance of mental ill-health as a precursor of suicide had already been published before this study was carried out. A study in which a doctor interviewed surviving relatives of 420 Parisians who had killed themselves concluded that suicide resulted from alcoholism, ill-health, bereavement, misery and poverty (Serin, 1926). The importance of Serin's work was recognised and made use of by Halbwachs (1930) in his book on suicide. Halbwachs, a pupil of Durkheim, saw that his teacher had overemphasised the importance of social determinants of suicide by neglecting the sick individual. Halbwachs devotes a chapter to the characteristics of people who commit suicide, drawing heavily on Serin's Paris study, emphasising the importance of mental abnormalities in suicide.

Sainsbury (1955) found a raised prevalence of both mental and physical illness recorded in the coroners' notes for a sample of suicides in London. Some 50 per cent of his cases were mentally ill. In Bristol, Seager and Flood (1965) supplemented coroners' records with a search of hospital records, and found two-thirds of their cases of suicide to be mentally ill. Two studies from the United States of America which interviewed relatives of suicides after the death found even higher proportions of the suicides had been mentally ill. Dorpat and Ripley (1960) employed social workers to interview the relatives of 114 suicides occurring in Seattle and concluded all the cases of suicide had been mentally ill before they died. Robins and his colleagues in St Louis (Robins et al., 1959), using specially trained senior medical students for the same purpose, concluded that 94 per cent of their 134 cases of suicide were mentally ill. In each study depressive illness and alcoholism accounted for more than half the diagnoses.

The more closely the individual suicide has been examined in consecutive series—first coroners' records, then coroners' records and hospital notes, and then these two sources combined with interviewing witnesses—the higher the proportion of suicides with mental illness is found to be.

The work described in this chapter, carried out by a psychiatrist and two research psychiatric social workers, was based on suicides which occurred in the County of West Sussex or the County Borough of Portsmouth. This area comprised a densely built-up urban centre with a large working-class population, a retirement zone and holiday resort along the coast, a county town, and a rural community with dispersed farms, small towns and villages: in summary, a representative cross-section of southern England with a population of 600,000. The total of 100 suicides comprised two samples: 25 of 29 suicides who died in West Sussex during 1966 and 1967, and 75 consecutive suicides who died in West Sussex or Portsmouth in 1968. The same clinical material was collected for each sample, but social data for the sample of 75 only.

Not included were residents of the area who died in other parts of England or abroad. These would be expected to form some 10 per cent of the total deaths of residents from suicide, since a few take their lives while away from home. Some are on holiday. Others travel to save their relatives embarrassment, or to make use of a preferred method such as car exhaust in a lonely wood, drowning, or jumping from a high place. Also excluded were suicides who were visitors to the area, unless living there for more than 6 months, the period used in the census to define residence.

Members of the research team attended inquests on unnatural

deaths for which a suicide verdict was likely, the coroner's office letting us know beforehand of this possibility. Because the inquest is public anyone may attend. If the coroner returned a verdict of suicide the case was included in the study. The witness at the inquest who seemed likely to know most about the suicide was visited at home without previous warning, and interviewed about the deceased. This had been found the most satisfactory method of obtaining co-operation while minimising distress. Contact by telephone, letter, through the family doctor and introduction at the inquest itself had been found in a pilot test of method to produce a high percentage of refusals. Refusals were undesirable because the exclusion of cases could bias the results in unknown ways, limiting the generalisability of the findings.

In today's safety-first ethical climate, visiting without warning might well have been barred as unethical. Yet most informants thought the inquiry worthwhile and were pleased to have helped to increase knowledge about such a puzzling phenomenon as suicide. The benefit from the opportunity to unburden was usually obvious, perhaps even more in those at first a little reluctant to assist, an impression verified in those spouses followed up 5 years afterwards (Shepherd and Barraclough, 1974).

Of the principal witnesses, 83 were first-degree relatives of the suicide: spouse, parent, sibling or child. Fifty-four principal witnesses had been living with the suicide when the death occurred. Other informants, often family members, provided facts about the suicide's life unknown to the principal informant. The informants—relatives, friends, the general practitioner in 94 cases, psychiatrists, physicians, pathologists, pharmacists, social workers, ministers of religion, nurses; anyone in fact who had relevant information, and some who turned out to have none—averaged 4.5 for each case.

Documentary evidence was also examined. Executive Council medical cards, which contain the family doctor's record of treatment (99 cases), postmortem reports (99 cases), psychiatric hospital notes (59 cases), and general hospital notes (34 cases) were read. The 39 suicide notes were, on the whole, not especially helpful unless they contained obvious psychopathology.

Two hundred and fifty-two items of information, 130 concerned with the suicide's medical and psychiatric symptoms, signs and past history, were rated for each case. The interview, based on a standard questionnaire, permitted interviewers to use their own discretion in wording questions, when this seemed necessary, to maintain rapport with distressed witnesses or to probe a topic more deeply. The headings used in the questionnaire, with sample questions from each section, are given in Appendix 1. For each item, information obtained from all sources was recorded, and discussed at a joint conference of the three interviewers and coded according to predefined categories. Checks of reliability carried out by joint interviews, in which one interviewed the witness and both rated replies, showed an acceptable measure of agreement between the three interviewers (Bunch, Barraclough, Nelson and Sainsbury, 1971a).

To make a clinical diagnosis a panel of three consultant psychiatrists reviewed the written evidence about symptoms and signs of illness for each case, and a diagnosis based on predefined criteria was allocated if at least two of the panel independently agreed on it. The diagnostic criteria were those of the International Classification of Diseases (ICD) modified to accommodate the peculiarities of an inquiry where the 'patient' was missing. When there were two or more diagnoses, as there were in 13 instances, one was selected as the principal or the more important condition. The diagnosis of personality disorder, based on Schneider (1950), proved reliable, but the ICD classification of subgroups did not. Many people with personality disorder fitted into more than one of the ICD subgroups, others did not fit any.

To evaluate the social data a standard of comparison from the same population was required. A comparison group of 150 people, matched with the suicides for age plus or minus 5 years, sex, whether ever married, and area of residence, was selected by a random method from the patient registers of two large group general practices, one in Portsmouth and one in West Sussex. For convenience the comparison group will be called 'controls' from now on. Two of the subjects selected were found to be having psychiatric outpatient treatment, and they were replaced. One hundred and forty-nine of the 150 control subjects selected were interviewed. The 150th, who refused, was not replaced by someone more tractable. His family doctor supplied some of the missing information. We made an effort to obtain a high level of compliance because the substitution of refusals would bias the controls by excluding unusual people and social isolates, factors considered to be important in predisposing to suicide.

We interviewed the controls using the same questionnaire as that used for the suicides, with the omission of clinical items. Checks similar to those employed with the suicide interview, including joint interviews and interviewing an informant about the control subject, provided satisfactory measures of reliability and validity (Bunch *et al.*, 1971a).

SEX, AGE, AND MARITAL STATUS

The 100 suicides comprised 53 men and 47 women. Their ages ranged from 19 to 93 years with an average value of 52 years. When assessed on their legal marital status, the status used in the census, 31 were single, 46 married, 19 widowed and 4 divorced. Compared with the population in which they had lived, there was an over-representation of men, those over 45, and the single, widowed and divorced. These findings are to be expected from national statistics for suicide, and suggest the sample is not atypical.

The actual marital status frequently differed from the legal because many of the married were separated and some lived in *de facto* relationships. In one instance a divorced couple still lived together as man and wife. One or two of the 46 marriages could be regarded as stable.

PSYCHIATRIC DIAGNOSIS

Ninety-three of the 100 cases were judged to be mentally ill and given a diagnosis. The principal diagnoses were depression (70 cases), alcoholism (15 cases), schizophrenia (3 cases), phobic anxiety state (3 cases), barbiturate dependence (1 case) and schizoaffective psychosis (1 case) (Table 1.1). Abnormal personality was diagnosed in 27.

For 13 suicides there was more than one psychiatric diagnosis; in ten cases alcoholism coexisted with depression, and in three cases mood disorder, depression or anxiety, and barbiturate dependence were linked.

12

Table 1.1: Psychiatric Diagnosis for 100 Consecutive Suicides

Principal	Other	Number of cases
Depression	None	64
	Terminal cancer	2
	Non-malignant terminal illness	2
	Barbiturate dependence	1
	Dementia + barbiturate dependence	1
Alcoholism	None	4
	Depression	9
	Non-malignant terminal illness	1
	Depression + non-malignant terminal illness	1
Schizophrenia		3
Phobic anxiety state	None	2
	Barbiturate dependence	1
Barbiturate dependence		1
Acute schizoaffective psychosis		1
No psychiatric abnormality		7
TOTAL		100

Depression

Since depression was so frequent, the characteristics of the 64 cases (30 men and 34 women) with depression as the only diagnosis are described in some detail. Their mean age was 54 years, and three-quarters were over 45. They contained an excess of single and widowed people compared with the census population, and fewer married. A high proportion of the married were either separated or living unhappily with their spouse. Their symptoms were similar to those of depressives seen in hospital practice, the most common being insomnia, sadness, weight change, difficulty in working, loss of interest, pessimism about the future, anorexia, reduction in activities and loss of energy.

Many cases had histories of previous mental disorder severe enough to require treatment. Thirty-three of the 64 had been referred to psychiatric services in the past and a further twelve were judged, on the evidence of witnesses, to have had previous depressive episodes which had not been treated by a psychiatrist, although some had had treatment from their family doctors. Eleven had a bipolar affective psychosis, as indicated by a past history of mania requiring psychiatric treatment. Twenty-one

13

had previous attempts at suicide documented in their records, and another eight had told a witness of a previous suicide attempt which had not been treated medically.

The following history illustrates a case of recurrent depression:

A 73-year-old man committed suicide by carbon monoxide poisoning from the domestic gas supply while his wife was on holiday.

The suicide's parents had good health and died in their 80s, but two sisters committed suicide some years before he did, presumably following a depressive illness although that was not known to us. His only son had had a depressive illness in middle age. The suicide had been a clerk, employed in the same job for 40 years until he retired early at 59 on account of depression. He had been married twice. The first marriage, a happy one, ended with his wife's death from cancer when he was 56, 5 years after his first episode of depression. He remarried at the age of 67. This marriage was reasonably happy when he was well, but there was friction when he was depressed.

The first attack of depression occurred when he was 51, and subsequently there were six more clear-cut episodes, all requiring treatment by a psychiatrist, and all remitting completely. Later episodes were longer than the earlier ones. He was said to have displayed behaviour consistent with a diagnosis of hypomania between episodes of depression, but this was not verified by a psychiatric interview. When not depressed, his personality was described as cheerful, active, outgoing, energetic, with a high self-regard: 'full of the joys of life'. He got up at 6 in the morning to do his gardening, and 'never had a worry'. He loved meeting people, going to dances and socials, belonged to several clubs and had a large circle of acquaintances.

For 2 years before his death he had complained of feeling depressed and generally unwell, losing interest in things, with no energy to do the gardening. He was slowed down, anxious, hypochondriacal, worried about poverty, thought people were against him and did not want him around. He had been attending a psychiatric day hospital off and on, and at the time of his death was taking 50 mg amitriptyline daily from his general practitioner. His wife thought there had been a definite improvement in his symptoms in the month before his death. No physical disease was found at postmortem.

This case illustrates an inherited predisposition to manic-depressive disease and perhaps to suicide as well, a possibility recently demonstrated in adoption studies. The social isolation from friends and acquaintances is the direct outcome of the effects of the illness, as is the impaired marriage. The dose of amitriptyline is below that recommended for continuing symptoms of a depressive illness.

A second history illustrates the bipolar form of the disease, with both depressive and clear-cut manic episodes:

A 49-year-old single woman, an inpatient in the rehabilitation unit of a psychiatric hospital, went missing from her ward about midday, and was later seen on a beach a few miles away, first pacing up and down at the water's edge, then running into the sea fully clothed. Her drowned body was subsequently recovered.

She had five older half-siblings, one of whom had had psychiatric treatment for a similar illness to hers. Her father, her mother's second husband, died before she was born, his cause of death unknown. Her mother's first husband had killed himself. The mother lived to be 85.

The suicide studied drama and then entered a branch of the armed forces, from which she was discharged at the age of 25 because of a mental illness, in retrospect probably the first of many hypomanic episodes, although at the time 'gross hysteria' appeared in the medical notes. A variety of clerical jobs followed discharge from the forces. Subsequent episodes of serious mental illness, requiring inpatient treatment, occurred when she was 44, 45 and 47; each time the diagnosis was depressive psychosis preceded by mania. To treat these episodes she had received ECT and imipramine for depression, haloperidol and phenothiazines for mania, and lithium for prophylaxis of both depression and mania. Three suicide attempts in the 5 years before she died are a measure of the intensity of the suicidal thinking which accompanied her depressed mood. Not all depressives think of suicide even when seriously ill. On the first occasion she jumped under a train, on the second swallowed weed-killer, and on the third ate berries she believed were poisonous.

15

When well her personality was described as sociable and bright, and because of her warmth she was able to make friends with ease. The frequent occurrence of swings of mood, 'either right down or right up', suggested the illness was rarely inactive, although clinically obvious in later life only. She loved to be the centre of attention, although was hypochondriacal about her physical health even when mentally well. Her interests were transitory but intense. There were many sexual relationships, with both men and women, but she never married or had children. At the time of her death she was without close relatives or friends nearby, her sister and a woman friend having moved away a year earlier.

For 19 months before the suicide she had been an inpatient in a mental hospital, making good progress on the rehabilitation ward. A week before she killed herself, nursing staff recalled a reduction in activity and speech, slowing down, loss of interest in her work in the library, and neglect of her appearance. She would shut herself in a cupboard and silently hide there in the darkness. The medication was thioridazine 50 mg daily.

Postmortem confirmed the cause of death to be drowning, and revealed no physical disease.

This case illustrates the destructive effect of recurrent bipolar mood disorder, and the predisposition to suicidal thoughts when depressed. The suicide of her mother's first husband can be conjectured as an influence there. The unstable mood, present from an early age and inaccessible to treatment, probably had a strong disruptive influence on the development of a mature personality, reflected in the absence of meaningful, close bonds with anyone at the time of her death. Rehabilitation wards are slow stream affairs designed for patients with severe but stable mental illnesses, principally schizophrenia, and may not always be suitable for those with relapsing manic-depressive disease.

Depressed suicides and living depressives compared

Since most episodes of depression do not end in suicide, identifying the type of depressive who is at higher risk of suicide is of practical value and theoretical interest. To advance this objective the 64 suicides with a principal diagnosis of depression, not associated with other psychiatric disorder or a serious medical condition, were compared with a sample of 318 patients with 'endogenous' depression (Barraclough and Pallis, 1975). This comparison aimed to detect characteristics which distinguished depressed suicides from depressives who had not killed themselves. Differences found would, it is assumed, be related to the fact of suicide.

The 318 depressives, a consecutive series referred for treatment to the Chichester District Psychiatric Service, had been studied to elucidate the differing effects of hospital- and community-based styles of psychiatric treatment. An examination of the reliability of diagnosis by National Health Service psychiatrists had been conducted in this inquiry, and the diagnosis of endogenous depression was known to be reliable (Sainsbury, 1971).

The comparison of suicides and depressives was carried out in two stages, first examining the distribution of age and sex using the 318 depressives, and second testing for clinical and social differences using a subsample composed of 128 of the 318 depressives. The subsample was drawn by selecting two depressives of the same sex and age as each suicide. Clinical and social factors are age- and sex-dependent, an effect removed by matching. Two depressives were selected for each suicide to increase the statistical power of the discrimination.

In the sample of 318 depressives, twice the number of women as men were referred for treatment of depression, but the ratio of women to men among the 64 depressed suicides was a good deal less, 34 to 30. This suggests that the suicide rate of male depressives is higher than that for female depressives, a phenomenon which may go some way to explaining the higher national suicide rate for men. This effect is to some extent counterbalanced, however, by the much higher prevalence of depression among women in the general population, which places more women than men at risk for suicide.

The age distribution of the male suicides was similar to that of the male depressives. In contrast, female suicides were somewhat older than female depressives. This age effect may help to explain the increasing incidence of suicide with advancing age for women, because the prevalence of depression in women increases with age, and also from these figures so does the risk of suicide for the female depressive. The effect of the prevalence of depression on the suicide rate is much greater in women than men, since a higher proportion of female suicides than male suicides are depressed, 72 per cent compared with 57 per cent in this study.

The next comparisons were carried out using the subsample of 128 living depressives, referred to as 'the depressives' from now on. There were significantly more single, and significantly fewer married, among the suicides than among the depressives. The special vulnerability of single people to suicide in middle age may in part be due to personality factors which prevent their marrying, and at the same time strengthen rather than weaken the bond with parents, so that the inevitable death of parents results in mood disorder and social isolation. This previously undescribed phenomenon is dealt with in more detail in Chapter 4 on social aspects, and in the paper by Bunch *et al.* (1971a). A further explanation may lie in the long-term effect of chronic and recurring illness preventing both marriage and a mature social circle, so increasing the risk of suicide when the resilience of youth is gone. The second of the two case descriptions given above illustrates the point. The high suicide rate for the divorced cannot be accounted for by an excess of the divorced among depressed suicides. The explanation is more likely to come from the special vulnerability of the alcoholic to suicide following marriage break-up. In contrast, the high suicide rate for the widowed is to some extent the outcome of widowhood being followed by recurrence of a depressive illness, in the new and unfamiliar social circumstances of living alone with altered responsibilities (Bunch, 1972).

In the literature about the depressed person most at risk for suicide, nearly all the symptoms of depression have been stated to be important. The majority of opinions, especially in textbooks, are based on uncontrolled clinical experience. In our study only three symptoms distinguished the suicides from the depressives: insomnia, impaired memory and self-neglect.

Insomnia had been present in some cases for years, as had its drug treatment with barbiturates, often the means of death. Insomnia and its drug treatment frequently antedated the fatal depressive episode, being for some a relic of a previous attack. Long nights of worried wakefulness can be understood as an experience likely to induce suicidal thinking. The finding underlines the importance of control of insomnia with effective and non-addictive drugs when treating a depressive illness.

Impaired memory probably results from the influence of mood disorder upon cognitive function.

Self-neglect is often a consequence of depressed mood, made worse by the poor morale which occurs when treatment is not progressing, especially in a setting of unhappy personal relationships or isolation.

The frequency distribution of other symptoms and signs was remarkable more for the similarity between the two groups than the differences. Not surprisingly the present episode of illness was much longer for the suicides than for the depressives.

Past histories of episodes of mental illness, and histories of mental illness in first-degree relations, were equally common in suicides and depressives. In striking contrast to the apparent similarity of the two groups on other clinical measurements, a history of a previous attempt at suicide was ten times more common for the suicides (41 per cent) as for the depressives (4 per cent).

These findings suggest that the suicides are clinically a fairly typical sample of depressives, except for a predisposition to have suicidal thinking when depressed, as shown by the histories of suicide attempts.

The similarity on clinical measurement of the two groups, apart from the tendency to suicidal thinking, suggests the explanation of suicide may be found in social circumstances. The most striking difference here was that seven times more suicides (42 per cent) than depressives (6 per cent) lived in one-person households. Living alone is closely linked with marital status, those living alone being predominantly single, widowed, divorced or separated. Sixty-three per cent of the suicides, compared with 39 per cent of depressives, were not currently married. The association between fatal depression, marital status and living alone may be the outcome of life events such as widowing and divorcing, which change the person's social environment and predispose to depression.

Equal proportions of each group lived in non-private households, hotels, boarding houses and institutions. Unselected samples of suicides always show an excess living in non-private households. That depressed suicides do not have the association suggests the association is with alcoholism and schizophrenia, and this was so in our study.

The other social features considered—occupational social class, employment status and urban or rural residence—did not distinguish the two groups.

To summarise, depressives who commit suicide are distinguished by sleep disturbance, a predisposition to think of self-harm, and an impoverished immediate social circle.

Alcoholism

Alcoholism characterised by long-standing heavy drinking with medical and social complications was the principal diagnosis for 15 of the 100 suicides (Table 1.2). With the aim of defining the features of the suicide-prone alcoholic, their clinical and social features are described and compared with those of an unselected group of alcoholics studied during a comprehensive survey of

Table 1.2: Symptoms for 15 Alcoholic Suicides

	No.	Percentage
Heavy drinking, causing physical or mental illness, or social disability	12	80
Heavy drinking, not causing such disability	3	20
Informant says suicide drank too much	15	100
Family says suicide drank too much	14	93
Suicide said he drank too much	6	40
Frequency of drinking:		
Daily	8	67
Two or three times weekly	5	33
Bout drinking	12	80
Physical illness due to drink	7	47
Trouble at work through drink	8	53
Arrested because of drunkenness	5	33
Heavy drinking at time of suicide	7	47
Recent change in drinking habits		
Increase	6	40
Decrease	8	53
Help to stop drinking	6	40
Duration of heavy drinking (years)		
0– 9	1	7
10–19	3	20
20–29	6	40
30–39	4	27
40–49	1	7
Age of onset of heavy drinking (years):		
10–19	5	33
20–29	7	47
30–39	1	7
40–49	1	7
50–59	0	0
60–69	1	7

alcoholism in Cambridgeshire (Moss and Beresford-Davies, 1967).

The twelve men and three women suicides with alcoholism gave a sex ratio similar to that of the Cambridgeshire survey, with an average age 10 years older than the Cambridgeshire group. Divorce and widowhood, commoner among the alcoholic suicides than the general population, the Cambridgeshire alcoholics or the 85 non-alcoholic suicides, does not include the separations for those still legally married, or convey the profoundly unhappy relations of those living with their spouses.

All 15 had lengthy histories of heavy drinking, the mean duration being 25 years. All but three began drinking before the age of 30. When classified according to Jellinek there were five chronic, five symptomatic, three uncontrolled and two bout drinkers. Half had previous histories of psychiatric care to control drinking, or to treat an affective disorder, histories similar to those of the Cambridgeshire group. In fact the many depressive symptoms resulted in nine of the 15 having a second diagnosis of depressive illness. None had previous episodes of mania, in contrast to the depressives without alcoholism. Past attempts at suicide had occurred in two-thirds, compared to 10 per cent of the Cambridgeshire group. None of the alcoholics had family histories of alcoholism, but four had family histories of affective disorder.

In 12 of the 15 alcoholic suicides drinking seriously impaired health or social functioning. Seven had alcohol-related physical disease present at the time of death. The central nervous system had been affected at some time in nearly every case; four had had delirium tremens, five grand mal fits, in three memory was permanently impaired, one had peripheral neuritis. One man had undiagnosed liver failure when he died.

To summarise: early addiction to alcohol had led to physical damage, especially to the central nervous system. Depressive illness was common, its onset recent and in its clinical features similar to that of the depressed suicide. Compared with living alcoholics the alcoholic suicides were older, more likely to be divorced or widowed, and to have histories of attempts at suicide in the past.

The following case history describes how prolonged addiction to alcohol adversely influenced physical and mental health, and destroyed a career and a marriage:

A 47-year-old married man with four children died from

21

carbon monoxide poisoning, by placing a gas poker inside a plastic bag into which he put his head. Born into a comfortable middle-class family the suicide's childhood had been happy and stable, with success in early life, reaching a good level in his profession. Drinking began in his 20s, resulting in compulsory retirement 2 years before death because drinking had become uncontrolled. A lower-income clerical post with poor status followed. After a drunken driving conviction he lost his licence and had to be driven about. The marriage, at first happy, became marred by jealousy and physical violence.

Admission to an alcoholism unit, outpatient psychotherapy and calcium carbimide resulted in temporary improvements. He became depressed, frequently threatening suicide and behaving aggressively when drunk. Mental hospital readmission had been arranged but death intervened. His epilepsy, peripheral neuritis, gastritis, and behaviour suggesting dementia were each alcohol-induced.

A second history shows how alcoholism affected the life of a man with a personality disorder which prevented his becoming socialised:

A 51-year-old unmarried man found unconscious in a gutter died shortly after admission to hospital. Postmortem showed death from cardiorespiratory failure, resulting from barbiturate poisoning. The pathologist noted a gastrectomy and wedge resection of the lung.

Born in Glasgow to respectable working-class parents, the suicide left school at 14, first moving to London then joining the merchant navy. After the war, by jumping ship, he migrated to the USA. In 1955 the US authorities deported him to England. From then on his employment comprised short spells in the catering trade terminated by dismissal for drunkenness. In the 2 years before his death he had at least four jobs. Six days before death drunkenness resulted in dismissal from a live-in job as a waiter in a holiday camp where he had worked the previous 7 months. His whereabouts from then until his discovery in the gutter could not be discovered.

Heavy drinking, mainly in bouts, began at 20 and continued until shortly before death. Seven offences for drunkenness were known. Alcohol resulted in admission to a mental hospital with delirium tremens a year before he died. The peptic ulcer requiring gastrectomy and the tuberculosis requiring lung surgery were both alcohol-related diseases. Inquiries found no friends or relations.

Schizophrenia

Suicide for the schizophrenic tends to occur without warning, a fact recorded since the late nineteenth century. The three cases of schizophrenia and one of schizoaffective psychosis were all young and single. Of the two long-term inpatients, one lived in a rehabilitation ward, the other in a back ward. A third patient lived in a bedsitter, attending a day hospital sometimes. The fourth had been placed on a compulsory admission order but had not been admitted to hospital. None had made past attempts at suicide or talked of suicide.

All four suicides used a method which showed determination: hanging in a little-used public lavatory, drowning with a suitcase of stones tied to the wrist, a massive aspirin overdose while living alone, and crushing beneath a train. Their common features were unsatisfactory personal lives and living circumstances, and partly controlled psychoses. Two case histories illustrate some of the points:

A single 41-year-old man living in a psychiatric hospital went out after eating breakfast. His body, found at midday on a local beach after the tide had gone out, had a suitcase filled with pebbles tied to one wrist with a handkerchief. There was no suicide note.

Until aged 12 the suicide had been 'a cheery little boy', but then had a personality change, becoming sensitive, shy, reserved, withdrawn and over-aware of other people's opinions. He had one girl friend only, when in his mid-20s. After a promising start with a scholarship to Oxford and a good degree in physics, he worked as a research physicist.

The first episode of schizophrenia at 24, treated with insulin coma and ECT, remitted enough for him to work 7 more years. Then followed three attacks of schizophrenia in quick succession, each requiring hospital admission. As a result he lost his job and did not work again.

For 6 years before he died schizophrenia kept him compulsorily detained under the Mental Health Act (1959) in a mental hospital. To be near his brother he moved hospital some 5 months before death, and had two changes of ward within the new hospital. The last was to the rehabilitation ward where his drug treatment was a depot injection of fluphenazine, 50 mg monthly.

For some weeks hallucinatory voices and delusions were a preoccupation. He was restless, never sitting down except for meals or to write a letter, spending the time walking the grounds with a transistor radio plugged into his ear, possibly to counteract auditory hallucinations. He had been applying for jobs by post but, when offered an interview for the day of the suicide, withdrew.

The following case was given the diagnosis of schizoaffective psychosis:

A single man of 35 died by crushing under a train. He had no family history of psychiatric illness, and had been successful in his working life, gaining a university degree in electrical engineering and then being employed for 12 years. His personnel officer described his work as brilliant. He spent a week in a mental hospital with a diagnosis of 'mixed anxiety, depression and tension' immediately after leaving university, and in the following year had outpatient treatment for anxiety and 'inadequate personality' with dextroamphetamine. His personality was described as always the same — flat with no display of emotion, shy with no friends, dependable and reliable. He lived in a small boarding house for 2 years before his death, visiting his parents every 3 weeks.

For 2 days before death he had looked sad and anxious, slowed in movement and speech. He displayed delusions and ideas of reference, believing people were accusing him of murdering prostitutes and suggesting he should commit suicide. He said he saw people in the road with chloroform pads and nuclear disarmament posters, and believed they referred to him. The day before the suicide his doctor made an appointment for psychiatric outpatients. By the evening his behaviour was so disturbed that arrangements were made to admit him to hospital compulsorily under the Mental Health Act after the necessary documents had been completed. When the ambulance reached the hospital door he forced his way out and ran to the nearby railway line.

Phobic anxiety state

The three cases of phobic anxiety state, young married people with symptoms severe enough to interfere with domestic and working lives, had all seen psychiatrists in the past and still required daytime sedation for symptom control. The two women were dependent on barbiturates, and the man took benzodiazepines and episodically drank alcohol in excess. All three killed themselves after unpleasant experiences affecting self-esteem: the loss of keenly anticipated jobs for two, the defection of a boyfriend for the third.

As well as these three with a primary diagnosis of phobic anxiety state, dependent on sedative drugs for symptom control, there were three women addicted to barbiturates, two with primary diagnoses of depression. These six cases share the common features of persistent experiences of unpleasant anxiety and depression only partly controlled by sedatives. The sedatives caused further symptoms and the social and inter-personal problems of drug abuse. The resemblance to the alcoholics, many of whom also abused sedative drugs, is close.

The following history illustrates some of the above points:

A married man of 38, living with his wife and seven children, killed himself with barbiturate and alcohol in the early hours of the morning, after writing a note in explanation.

After training to be a merchant navy officer and having some 12 successful years at sea the suicide developed a phobic anxiety state when aged 29. Symptoms began sharply and unexpectedly while eating in public, and never disappeared completely. The symptoms occurred when in the company of strangers, especially his superiors, and comprised anxiety, uncertainty and indecision with sweating, palpitations and shaking. The shaking prevented his signing documents in front of people or doing chart work while observed. At home among friends and family the symptoms were minimal, only to recur when he returned to sea. He coped in part by avoiding anxiety-provoking situations such as eating with passengers, and by the sensible use of sedatives.

Psychiatric treatment including psychotherapy, benzo-diazepines, phenelzine and tricyclic antidepressants had not succeeded. Barbiturates relieved symptoms better than other sedatives. Alcohol may have been used for symptom control, since he drank too much in bouts lasting a few days.

The day before death his employers had rebuked him and delayed an anticipated promotion, alleging poor performance on the previous voyage. He responded with anger and distress, but not obvious depression nor talk of suicide, which was unexpected.

A feature of this disorder, inability to cope with criticism without unusually severe reactions ranging from disappointment to despair depending on the significance of the criticism, may have induced a sharp and severe mood of black despair in this man. Other evidence suggested poor self-esteem which would make coping with criticism that much more difficult.

Not mentally ill

Of the seven suicides classified as not mentally ill, only one was entirely without symptoms or signs of psychiatric illness — perhaps an indication of a conservative diagnostic approach. For the other six classified as not mentally ill the evidence was to some extent inconclusive, as the following two cases show:

A retired unmarried state registered nurse, aged 77, lived reclusively in a rented bedsitting room. No relatives or friends could be found after she died, and virtually nothing of her early life was known. The landlady looked after her well. In spite of age, her physical and mental health had been good until 10 days before she died, when continuous abdominal pain began. The general practitioner prescribed conservative treatment. The pain continued; she could not eat and lost weight, and hinted she had cancer. Arrangements for transfer to a nursing home, so the landlady could have a fortnight's holiday, were made, but the suicide asphyxiated herself with a plastic bag before arrangements were completed. An abscess in the pouch of Douglas, arising from a ruptured diverticulosis coli and pelvic peritonitis, uncovered at postmortem, explained the abdominal symptoms.

A prosperous 72-year-old childless retired civil engineer

lived with his wife in a seaside suburb for 16 years after early retirement. His physical and mental health had always been good until glaucoma made eye surgery necessary a year before his suicide. He spoke about fears of blindness to his family doctor and ophthalmologist, who reassured him that his sight was not in danger. But he remained preoccupied with thoughts of impending blindness. His wife, who was not aware of his worry, could not remember his showing any signs of illness or complaining of symptoms. He died from domestic gas poisoning without giving any warning of his plans or leaving a note.

These two cases share the features of advanced age, no children, few relatives, and physical disease which possibly formed a basis for hypochondriacal delusions. In both cases the witnesses interviewed seemed poorly informed, so symptoms of mental illness may have been present but not observed.

The following case was the only example of 'rational' suicide following an appraisal of future prospects, without good evidence of a depressive illness:

A medical practitioner of 65 lived alone in a flat to which she had moved from London 2 months before her suicide. The moved resulted from a wish to be near family following her husband's death 8 months before. After qualifying, the suicide, who came from a medical family, practised abroad successfully, returning to England 10 years before her death, at which time she was working part-time on medical translation. Her marriage at 40 was happy, although childless.

Her mental health had been sound, as had her family's. In contrast her physical health was impaired. Coronary artery disease, confirmed at postmortem, caused a myocardial infarction 18 months before death. Angina continued, limiting activity and vitality. Menière's disease, present for 10 years, and treated with three separate operations, left a residuum of impaired balance and complete deafness in one ear.

She spoke of suicide, emphasising her widowed loneliness, and the future, as she saw it, of declining health. Before taking an overdose of a fast-acting barbiturate she put her affairs in order, including instructions about the funeral.

27

PERSONALITY

Using a definition based upon Schneider's concept, 27 of the 100 suicides had an abnormal personality. Broadly speaking, the definition required persistent behaviour harmful to the subject or other people, not caused by illness. In 20 of the 27 all three psychiatrists agreed on the classification, a reassuringly high reliability for an imprecise definition. The reliability of an alternative classification based on the ICD proved too low for use.

Personality plays an important part in suicide, as may be seen in case histories. Response to both physical and mental illness is determined in part by personality factors. Predisposition to mental illness is believed to be associated with certain personality types, for example schizoid personality and schizophrenia, and cyclothymic personality and bipolar manic-depressive disorder. This point is illustrated in the case histories of schizophrenia and manic-depressive psychosis given above. Some of the social circumstances found in association with suicide result from personality traits, for example living alone by choice. Living alone seems to place people at risk for suicide when they become ill. The case history of the nurse, above, demonstrates the point. Living alone for other people is involuntary, the result of bereavement or a marriage break-up. Coping ability, an aspect of personality, has an important bearing on the outcome of the new living circumstances. The case history of the widowed doctor is an example, and other examples are given in the section describing the effect of parental bereavement (Chapter 4). Personality may also cause some of the distressing circumstances which are so frequently found preceding suicide, and the same personality traits may determine response to the self-determined distressing situation, especially mood disturbance and drug or alcohol abuse, as can be seen from the second case history in the section on alcoholism.

THREATS AND WARNINGS OF SUICIDE

There used to be a reassuring belief that those who spoke of suicide rarely killed themselves. This is now known, from the evidence of relatives of suicides, to be untrue. Our findings about warnings are similar to those of Robins et al. (1959). Unequivocal statements about intending to kill themselves were made, according to witnesses, by 34 of the 100 suicides during the year before they died. For example one man said, when threatened with a court appearance for a crime of which he was almost certainly guilty, 'I will kill myself rather than appear', and he did. The alcoholics gave stark warnings more often than other diagnostic groups. The schizophrenics gave none.

If more ambiguous statements about death are counted, for example as one depressive said, 'You'll have my gratuity — I won't be here', 21 more cases had given warnings, a total of 55 per cent. This proportion probably underestimates warnings, since not every possible witness was interviewed. A third of those who gave warnings did so more than a month before death, indicating that there would have been time for preventive action. Suicide has a gestation period, especially for the depressive.

Threats of suicide may be a cry for help as fashion, at least until recently, has insisted. But this may be too simple, for threats can be a statement of fact, evidence of a conflict between the wish to live or die, or frankly coercive, as well as the cry for help postulated by Stengel (1963) and others.

Clinical experience, however, shows that few of those who think and talk about suicide go on to commit it. The value of the finding is in laying to rest a myth, and in giving confidence to the clinician to find out from patients if they are experiencing thoughts of suicide, which can give relief. I think it unlikely that suicide occurs without the person having earlier thoughts of it, the exceptions being those few patients with serious psychoses who may not realise they are going to die from their actions, and the rare impulsive act, of which there was no obvious example in our 100.

CONTACT WITH FAMILY DOCTORS AND PSYCHIATRISTS

To what extent are suicides in contact with doctors?

Fifty-nine of the 100 suicides had seen their family doctor in the month before they died, and 40 within 7 days of their death. The figures for the control group were many times lower, 17 per cent and 7 per cent. Of the 17 suicides who had not seen their family doctor for more than a year, three were long-stay patients in a mental hospital and one, a general practitioner, was her own doctor.

Contact as a psychiatric patient was less straightforward to determine. The definition of a psychiatric patient included current inpatients and those who had seen a psychiatrist within 3 months of death as outpatients, unless the case notes showed that the patient had been discharged from treatment, or that the time to the next arranged appointment was to be longer than 3 months. This operational definition eliminated those who had failed outpatient appointments yet remained on the 'books'. This definition gave 24 suicides under psychiatric care — five inpatients and 19 outpatients. Eleven of the 24 had seen their psychiatrist in the 7 days before the suicide; 18 in the month before they died.

The suicides under psychiatric care were those with the more severe illnesses: the three with schizophrenia, nearly all the bipolar affective disorders and the difficult alcoholics. Of the 76 not under psychiatric care, two had been discharged shortly before their suicide and one was in the process of compulsory admission.

Accumulating these findings shows 48 suicides had seen a doctor within 7 days of death and 69 within the month. Medical opportunity for prevention was there, if prevention were possible.

PSYCHOTROPIC DRUG TREATMENT AND ECT

To appraise scope for improvement in preventive measures the physical treatments were examined.

The term psychotropic drug used here means drugs prescribed to alter mental state beneficially, and to control unwanted behaviour arising from mental illness. The interviews with doctors and the medical records provided the facts about prescribed treatment, but whether the prescribed drug was taken as instructed could not be known with certainty.

Eighty-two suicides had been prescribed one or more psychotropic drugs in the recent past. Sixty-four had drugs for insomnia; for 53 this drug was a barbiturate (Table 1.3). Many suicides used their barbiturates for daytime sedation and some doctors prescribed it for that purpose. Barbiturates are dangerous used in this way. They become less effective over time so more is taken. Patients become addicted. If they try to give up they mistake withdrawal symptoms for a return of the original disorder and increase the dose. When taken in doses only a little beyond the therapeutic, barbiturates cause confusion and aggressiveness, and impair coordination, making matters worse rather than better. Benzodiazepines, their contemporary successors, have the same disadvantages. Barbiturates, unlike benzodiazepines, are rapidly fatal in overdose, especially with alcohol. Fifty-six of the 100 suicides died from poisoning, and 45 of the 56 from barbiturate poisoning.

In the first of the following case histories the medication was out of control, and the second illustrates irresponsible prescribing:

A 76-year-old childless married woman was staying with her sister, while her husband had his gall-bladder removed. For 10 years she had taken 400 mg of quinalbarbitone each night, and for the previous 2 years unknown but substantial amounts of barbiturate during the day as well. According to her general practitioner she stole her husband's amylobarbitone, and illegally obtained sedative drugs from other doctors. Drugs were also begged from her sister. The clinical picture was of depression and mild dementia, with some confusion, probably due to the barbiturates. Attempts to switch to sedatives other than barbiturates had failed. She died from a barbiturate overdose.

A 45-year-old single woman had lived alone since the recent death of both her parents. She was drawing sick benefit on psychiatric grounds but was actively looking for work in a stables. In the previous 7 years there had been four admissions for agitated depression with a reasonable response to treatment. At the time of her suicide from a barbiturate overdose the drug treatment was 100 mg of amitriptyline and 1 g of amylobarbitone a day, some five to ten times the recommended dose of barbiturate and indicative of tolerance. This prescribing, recorded for the previous 6 months, had probably been going on for a year. The general practitioner had not seen the suicide for 7 months and the receptionist gave fresh prescriptions on demand.

Of the 64 suicides with uncomplicated depressive illnesses discussed earlier in this chapter, only 19 were prescribed antidepressant drugs. A trial of treatment with antidepressants, indicated by the diagnosis, would have been feasible because the suicide had recently seen a doctor.

31

This, the principal evidence that medical treatment could prevent suicide, is undermined by the fact that 19 of the 64 suicides with uncomplicated depressive illnesses were prescribed antidepressant drugs. Why had these drugs failed to prevent the death? A more detailed description suggests the failure does not seriously weaken the argument.

Monoamine oxidase inhibitors (MAOI) had been prescribed for four cases, and tricyclic antidepressants drugs for 15. The four prescribed MAOI were all severe cases for which such drugs are not effective. The following case illustrates the point:

> A 50-year-old man, with a recurring bipolar manic-depressive illness which had begun in his 20s, had a recurrence of depressive symptoms after a lengthy remission during which he had not needed psychiatric treatment. His general practitioner, whom he consulted shortly after his final recurrence began, and who knew his history, prescribed tranylcypromine and barbiturate. There was no improvement, though he had improved in the past with tricyclics and with ECT. He killed himself with the barbiturates.

Of the 15 cases prescribed tricyclic antidepressants, five had failed the treatment because they had taken the same drug for more than 6 months without improvement. In four others where there was little improvement with antidepressant drugs ECT had been started, the suicide occurring at the beginning of the course. The drug could not be concluded to have failed in these nine cases, because the average dose used was well below that recommended for psychiatric practice. In four other cases the relatives were sure of non-compliance, and in another the drug had only been started the day before the suicide. In only one instance was there evidence of improvement with a tricyclic before death.

Thus in nine cases the drug had apparently failed, in some probably because the dose was not high enough, in five it had not had an adequate trial, and in four an MAOI had been prescribed when a tricyclic was indicated. The low-dose treatment is a feature of the difference between family and psychiatric practice in the use of antidepressants.

Electroconvulsive treatment was under-used. In several cases previous episodes of depression had been successfully treated with ECT, but ECT had started for only four of the recurrences

Table 1.3: Prescribed Psychiatric Treatment at the Time of Death for 100 Consecutive Suicides (percentages)

	All (n = 100)	Depression (n = 64)	Alcoholism (n = 15)	Miscellaneous (n = 14)	Not mentally ill (n = 7)
Any drug	82	81	87	100	43
Any hypnotic	64	70	73	43	29
Barbiturates	53	53	53	57	43
Antidepressants	21	30	7	7	—
Phenothiazines	21	20	20	36	—
Minor tranquillisers	21	23	20	21	—
Halperidol	1	2	—	—	—
Calcium carbimide	1	—	7	—	—
ECT	3	5	—	7	—

which preceded the suicide. It was clear that both patient and doctor disliked repeating ECT.

Lithium prophylaxis of recurring episodes of depression and mania has become essential to the successful management of this dreadful disease. The key trial of the value of lithium in prophylaxis had not been published at the time of our inquiry, and the use of lithium depended on the doctor's view of controversial evidence. Only one suicide had been prescribed lithium. The potential of lithium treatment for suicide prevention is discussed in Chapter 8, and illustrated by the case history in Appendix 2.

The purpose of this part of the inquiry, to evaluate the physical methods of treatment prescribed against recommended optimal standards, carries a danger that in reaching a judgement, with the help of informed hindsight, the inherent difficulty of successful treatment of the mentally ill is overlooked and foolish conclusions reached. Nevertheless, the results do support the view that doctors prescribed dangerously large amounts of sedatives, especially barbiturates, and dangerously small amounts of antidepressant treatment, including ECT.

Barbiturates, then prescribed without restriction just as benzodiazepines are now, caused 30 per cent of the deaths of the 4,500 suicides occurring in England and Wales each year, and they killed 46 of the 100 suicides in this series. Antidepressants, available some 10 years, had not become widely used in family practice, in part the result of the utter neglect of psychiatry in English medical schools, now largely remedied.

DISCUSSION AND CONCLUSIONS

The most striking finding, the high percentage of suicides (93 per cent) who were mentally ill at the time they died, could be an artefact resulting from bias on the part of coroners, informants, interviewers or the psychiatrists making the diagnoses.

Coroners, it can be argued, bring in a verdict of suicide when there is evidence of present or past mental illness, allocating other suicides to the open verdict or accidental death categories, thereby inflating the proportion of mentally ill suicides. Similarly they may allocate accidental deaths with evidence of mental illness to the suicide category. Neither form of systematic bias is likely because English coroners, nearly all of whom are lawyers and trained to weigh evidence, are required to use a legal definition of suicide which relies almost exclusively on evidence of intent. Their decisions are open to appeal, which should make them careful. Shortly after our inquiry started an important appeal against a suicide verdict, the first for 10 years, reiterated the requirement that verdicts should rest on positive evidence of intent to die and not on the coroner's surmise (Jennings and Barraclough, 1980). Our three coroners, all lawyers, referred to the decision, suggesting an influence on their practice. Nevertheless there were three among the 100 cases where an accidental death verdict seemed more correct to us than suicide. Two were mentally ill, so the proportion of the 100 diagnosed as mentally ill does not change if they are removed. We did not collect evidence on open verdict and accidental death cases, so could not decide about suicides misclassified there.

Relatives might overestimate evidence of mental illness to explain or justify the suicide. The interviewers' observations suggested this to be rare. Relatives often emphasised the suicide's mind had been lucid, and some objected to the coroner's rider 'suicide while the balance of the mind was disturbed'.

Interview bias was minimised by preparing definitions of all recorded items beforehand and scoring items positively if the three interviewers agreed the evidence to be strong enough. The three psychiatrists who decided whether mental illness had been present used written definitions of diagnoses, and the level of agreement between them was satisfactory. The case histories of those classified 'not mentally ill' suggest conservative diagnostic standards.

Documentary evidence collected before the suicide is free of subjective bias. Two-thirds of the cases had a documented past history of mental illness and/or attempted suicide. Their symptom pattern and family histories were similar to those of an unselected series of living depressives. The psychotropic drugs prescribed for 83 per cent showed that a doctor had diagnosed treatable psychological symptoms or mental illness.

The finding of mental illness in nearly all cases does not therefore represent bias in the collection or the interpretation of clinical observation, but is apparently valid, a conclusion supported by similarity to the results of four other studies using comparable methods (Dorpat and Ripley, 1960; Robins *et al.*,

1959; Bagley, Jacobson and Rehin, 1976; Chynoweth, Tonge and Armstrong, 1980) (Table 1.4).

Table 1.4: Main Psychiatric Diagnoses in Three Series of Suicides (percentages)

	Barraclough *et al.* (1974) (*n* = 100)	Dorpat and Ripley (1960) (*n* = 108)	Robins *et al.* (1959) (*n* = 134)
Depression	70	28	47
Alcoholism	15	26	25
Schizophrenia	4	11	2
Other	4	35	20
Not mentally ill	7	—	6

Though the mentally ill have a high rate of suicide — for example Guze and Robins (1970) report 15 per cent eventually die by suicide, compared to the general population figure of less than 1 per cent — only a minority of the mentally ill kill themselves. Those who do may have special distinguishing characteristics which, if recognised, could prompt preventive action. The comparison between the depressed suicides and living depressives did not reveal striking differences in symptoms, except for many more suicide attempts. This might just as well reflect differences in personality, cultural background or social circumstances as differences in type of depressive illness. The importance of social factors is shown by the suicides being more likely to live alone, and to be unmarried or have broken marriages.

Drug treatment, the only form of medical intervention we subjected to detailed examination, had frequently been inadequate. A minority only of the depressives were prescribed antidepressants, especially under-used in depression complicated by alcoholism or physical illness. Even when used, the doses of antidepressant were lower than optimal. In contrast to the under-use of antidepressants, the prescription of hypnotics and sedatives had been excessive, often providing the means of overdose. There was clearly scope for more appropriate use of physical methods, including ECT, for the treatment of depressive illness.

2

Physical Illness and Suicide

Physical illness is believed to play a part in the chain of events preceding suicide, and many writers on the subject have commented on this likelihood — Durkheim being a notable exception. A useful review is provided by Whitlock (1986), from which the conclusion can be drawn that there is a relationship, its nature uncertain.

INTRODUCTION

On theoretical grounds a link between physical illness and suicide might be expected for a number of reasons. Patients who know they are going to die from an incurable disease, terminal cancer for example, may decide that pre-empting a natural death is the less horrible alternative. Some physical disease may be especially difficult to bear because of disfigurement, disability, pain or discomfort — symptoms which may make the sufferer feel death is better than life. The scientific evidence for such 'rational' suicide in Western culture is slim.

The physiological influence of disease on mood, and the effect of disease-induced handicap on social circumstances, are more plausible theories. The metabolic effects of physical disorders, such as hypothyroidism, may cause depressive illness, as may the metabolic influence of medicines used in the treatment of physical disorders — antihypertensive drugs and corticosteroids for instance. The neuropathology of some diseases may cause mood disorders, and also alter behaviour, producing social stresses or interpersonal problems which themselves then become important factors in causing suicide.

Multiple sclerosis and traumatic brain injury are good examples. Physical disease and its surgical treatment, mastectomy for example, might act as a stressful event predisposing to depression. Disease interfering with sight, hearing, speech or mobility might increase isolation and loneliness, factors considered important in the causation of suicide. Certain behaviours, for example abuse of alcohol and drugs, which themselves have high suicide rates, also increase risk for some physical and psychiatric disorders, resulting in an indirect relation between a physical disease and suicide. The chance conjunction of any physical disease, or its treatment, and a depressive illness might result in a suicide which would not have occurred in an uncomplicated depression. There are therefore quite strong theoretical reasons why physical disease should increase risk of suicide.

The evidence for a link between physical disease and suicide derives from studies of two kinds: long-term follow-up studies to establish suicide rates for individual physical diseases, and case studies of consecutive series of suicides to measure prevalence of physical disease. A higher suicide rate for a group of people with a disease than for the general population, or an increased prevalence of a disease in a group of suicides as assessed by comparison with a control group, would establish a statistical association suggesting that physical disease plays a part in causing suicide. The long-term follow-up has the statistical advantage of a large number of cases, increasing confidence in the result, but the disadvantage of not being able to trace the effect of the disease on predisposition to suicide for the individual. It is of greater value for studying the suicide rate of a single disease. The case study approach suffers from the statistical disadvantage of small numbers, but the important advantage of being able to see more clearly the origin and effect of a disease. Because of the smaller numbers it is useful mainly for establishing a relation between suicide and physical disease considered as a whole, or physical diseases grouped because of some common attribute.

Both approaches require a standard to assess the significance of findings. National suicide rates are suitable for the long-term follow-up. Special control or comparison groups are needed for the case study approach. A problem is the postmortem findings which provide facts for the suicide group, which cannot be provided for a living control group. A solution might be a group of dead people who have had postmortems, but reflection shows that any group which has been autopsied is far from the random sample required.

Of the many papers on the relation between physical illness and suicide only one (Jones, 1965) has tested the hypotheses using consecutive suicides and age/sex-matched controls selected by a random method. Jones used hospital treatment as the measure of illness. The 17 male suicides in his study had significantly more hospital treatment for serious physical disease than the 170 male controls. The 13 female suicides had more hospital treatment than the 130 female controls also, but the difference was not statistically significant. The result of one study of 30 cases is probably insufficient for a conclusion.

Our study aimed to discover if serious physical disease and handicap were more common in the sample of suicides than among the age- and sex-matched 'control' group of people without mental illness, described in Chapter 1. The need for a control group shows that the importance of physical illness is less obvious than that of mental illness, which is so common in suicide that a control is not needed to be sure there is an excess.

The case histories of the physically ill suicides made clear that mood disorder was usually present, as well as the physical disease, as in the following examples:

A 66-year-old retired railway engine driver lived with his wife. Throughout his adult life, ups and down of mood periodically affected his behaviour: he was at times phobic about underground travel, and outspokenly overconcerned about his health. There was no family history of mental illness. A minor railway accident just before his retirement caused him to take a year off work, the condition being diagnosed 'neurasthenia' by his family doctor. Shortly before his death he suffered recurrent pulmonary emboli, undiagnosed antemortem, with haemoptyses and dyspnoea. Then, quite suddenly, he developed a severe agitated depressive illness when he said he thought he might have lung cancer. A fortnight later he shot himself.

A 93-year-old widower had lived alone in a seaside hotel for 15 years since his wife's death. His life had been a good one: a happy marriage, a family of successful children, commercial prosperity in middle life, and a circle of friends who liked and respected him. He had successfully coped with a series of crises — migration to the East when young, near-bankruptcy in late middle age, and finally loneliness, widowhood and financial dependency. Shortly before his suicide by asphyxiation, an agitated depressive illness suddenly began. At postmortem a large gastric carcinoma, unsuspected during life, was found. His brother had had a severe mental illness in middle life.

A word of explanation is required on evaluating the findings about physical illness. An exact evaluation of the health status of suicides by comparison with a group of living subjects presents insoluble problems. The suicides are beyond interrogation, so their personal experience of disease can never be completely known, nor can they be physically examined or investigated. Paradoxically the autopsy may reveal unreported or unknown disease for which there is no completely satisfactory standard of evaluation.

Yet by taking aspects of disease and of handicap which can be reliably and validly measured for both suicide and control, ideally by documentary evidence completed before the suicide occurred, an approach can be made to the testing of some specific hypotheses about the prevalence of disease and the effects of disease in each group.

METHOD

Hypotheses were tested by comparing the prevalence of physical disease and its effects in 75 of the suicides and the 150 controls described in Chapter 1. The method employed is briefly restated, to emphasise the techniques used to assess physical illness.

The relatives and friends of 75 consecutive suicides were questioned, soon after the death, about the dead person's present and past physical health. We interviewed the general practitioner, read his record of treatment (the Executive Council's medical card) and hospital records of recent medical treatment. Private practitioners recently consulted were written to. The reports of the 75 coroners' postmortems supplemented these facts, usually confirming suspected pathology, but sometimes refuting it, and occasionally revealing unknown disease.

We assessed the 150 controls in the same way, except that they were interviewed directly. The general practitioners' records of treatment and hospital records were scrutinised, and private doctors recently consulted were contacted. To check that interviewing people about themselves produces not too dissimilar results to those obtained by interviewing a witness, as for the suicides, we interviewed a near-relative of 23 (15 per cent) controls selected by a random method, and found 95 per cent of the relatives' answers agreed with those of the controls.

To assess the physical illness a consultant physician reviewed the notes of each suicide and of each control. He decided if the subjects suffered from significant physical disease, made a diagnosis if they did, and then assigned a rating of medical seriousness as follows:

Terminal cancer
Terminal non-malignant disease
Other cancer
Other serious non-malignant disease
Non-serious disease
Apparently healthy

RESULTS

If suicide was a common choice of the terminally ill, more suicides than controls should have terminal disease. Three suicides (3 per cent) had terminal disease which was known before their deaths, compared with five controls (3 per cent). This finding suggests that terminal disease plays a negligible part in determining suicide by pre-emption of natural death, as suggested in the introduction to this Chapter.

Two more suicides were discovered, at postmortem, to have disease which would have rapidly killed them. If there were no covert terminal disease in the control group, this small and statistically insignificant excess of terminal disease in the suicides is consistent more with a non-cognitive influence on predisposition to suicide, perhaps a physiological influence on mood.

Those rated as apparently healthy comprised 41 per cent of the suicides and 43 per cent of the controls — remarkably similar proportions.

Conditions rated as serious, that is 'other cancers' and 'other serious non-malignant disease', were present in rather more of the suicides (33 per cent) than controls (25 per cent), although the difference is not of statistical significance. Less serious disease was present in 21 per cent of suicides and 28 per cent of controls.

Since none of the differences between the two groups is of statistical significance, the two groups appear to be comparable on those measures of severity of physical disease identified before the suicide. There may be a trend towards the suicides having rather more serious disorders, but a trend which cannot be identified on a group of this size is too small to be of practical importance.

The presence of more than one disease may be a greater stress than a single condition, and in that way predispose to suicide. Thirty-one per cent of suicides and 31 per cent of controls had one disease diagnosed, 19 per cent and 15 per cent two, and 5 per cent and 10 per cent three or more. The two groups therefore have a similar frequency of multiple disease, though this comparison gives no weight to the severity of the diseases present. The three suicides and five controls with terminal disease each had one other disease of significance. Of the combined group with 'other cancers' and 'other serious disease', eleven suicides and 23 controls had one 'other serious disease' as well. The two groups seem similar on these measures too.

Diagnosis

Although the two groups do appear to be equivalent on measures of medical severity of the diseases present, there may still be differences of distribution of diagnosis. Since there were too few cases to test for an association with every conceivable diagnosis, the diseases diagnosed were grouped into the systems classification of the International Classification of Diseases. When compared on the frequency of diseases of all degrees of severity, suicides and controls had similar proportions in each of the major groupings. However when the 'non-serious' diseases were removed from the comparison, five suicides and no controls had disorders of the digestive system (ICD Group IX). This is a statistically significant difference of frequency (chi-square 7.4; d.f.=1; $p<0.01$). A difference at a probability of 1 per cent would be expected by chance at least once from the 44 chi-square tests used to examine these data, so not too much weight can be placed on the statistical association alone. However the case-control method allows cases that contribute to a statistical excess to be examined. Consideration of the clinical histories shows the association is most unlikely to be a statistical artefact:

Case 1. A 62-year-old man had been an alcoholic for 45 years and was known to have alcoholic cirrhosis. He had a long-standing depressive illness with much anxiety and appeared to drink to relieve the symptoms. Autopsy showed evidence of liver failure. His relative's observations about behaviour supported a diagnosis of hepatic encephalopathy.

Case 2. A 39-year-old man had been alcoholic since his teens. Behaviour suggestive of personality disorder and recurring episodes of depression were long-standing features. Four years before his suicide a duodenal ulcer was treated with a gastroenterostomy and vagotomy. Abdominal pain and discomfort present before his death were thought to have been caused by a stomal ulcer, but this was not confirmed at autopsy.

Case 3. A 54-year-old man developed symptoms of a depressive illness and a peptic ulcer shortly after his wife died. He killed himself 11 weeks after her death. Autopsy showed an acute peptic ulcer.

Case 4. A 93-year-old man had been in good health all his life until a few months before his suicide, when an agitated depression developed. He was under threat of eviction because of insufficient funds. Concurrent abdominal symptoms led to a diagnosis of gastritis. Autopsy showed inoperable gastric carcinoma.

Case 5. A 38-year-old man had schizophrenia of 20 years duration. Shortly before his death he had an attack of biliary colic which settled without surgery. Autopsy showed gall stones and a contracted gall bladder.

These case studies suggest there is a real if indirect association between digestive system disorders and suicide. Addiction to alcohol combined with mood disorder is the cause of the link in

43

Cases 1 and 2. Alcohol excess may result in cirrhosis and peptic ulcer, and it also predisposes to suicide. In Case 3 the acute effect of bereavement may be conjectured to have resulted in peptic ulceration; and widowhood has a high suicide rate. In Case 4 the gastric cancer may, by unknown metabolic influences, have caused the mood disorder, or predisposed to its development, or it may have been incidental. Only in Case 5 does the association, between gall stones and suicide, appear fortuitous.

The probability of an association between suicide and peptic ulcer is strengthened by the fact that two more alcoholic suicides, making three in all, had had gastrectomies, and four other suicides, all with depression, had been treated in the past for peptic ulcer. Three controls had histories of gastrectomy and four others of treatment for peptic ulceration. The suicides therefore had twice the frequency of ulcer history as the controls. This difference, although not statistically significant, does corroborate the conclusions of the literature review (Whitlock, 1986) showing a high suicide rate for peptic ulceration.

Central nervous system (CNS) disease, which might be conjectured as especially likely to predispose to suicide, was only a little more common in suicides than in controls, except for epilepsy which was significantly more frequent. Three suicides had CNS disorders diagnosed before death; multiple sclerosis, dominant-side hemiplegia as the result of a stroke, and posterior cerebellar artery syndrome. Five controls had CNS disorders: three cases of parkinsonism and two hemiplegias resulting from stroke. One other suicide had a cerebral contusion, caused by an old head injury, discovered at autopsy.

Epilepsy was present in five suicides compared with three controls. Three of the suicides were alcoholic, one a barbiturate addict, and the fifth, apparently mentally well, lived in the mental hospital to which he had been admitted 20 years before with an epileptic psychosis. The control epileptics, otherwise in good health, lived contented and productive lives. The relation between epilepsy and suicide is considered in Chapter 3.

Cancer, particularly terminal malignant disease, is believed to account for a proportion of suicides, in ways suggested in the introduction to this chapter. This belief is not supported here. One suicide had an operable rodent ulcer, another an inoperable gastric cancer only discovered at autopsy (Case 5 above). Three controls had cancers: oesophagus, prostate and disseminated carcinoma from an unknown primary site.

Handicap

Physical disease might predispose to suicide by causing pain, discomfort or disability, or loss of communication with others because of deafness, blindness or speech disorder. If this were so the 75 suicides should score higher on measures of these disease effects, which for convenience will be referred to collectively as handicap, than the 150 controls.

Pain had been persistently complained of by 32 (43 per cent) of the suicides and 32 (21 per cent) of the controls, a statistically significant difference of frequency (chi-square 12.0; d.f.=1; $p<0.001$). This finding does not necessarily mean that suicides had more painful conditions than controls. Nearly all the suicides complaining of pain had depressed mood, and pain is a common symptom of depression, often attached to a pre-existing condition. The equivalence of the two groups for physical disease, of all degrees of severity, including disorders of the musculoskeletal system which is a common source of pain in mood disorder, suggests depression is the likely explanation.

Discomfort, a measure of something less than pain, had been complained of by 23 (31 per cent) of the suicides and 53 (35 per cent) controls.

Suicides did not differ from controls on any of the five measures of locomotor disability used. Ten suicides (13 per cent) and 15 controls (10 per cent) had difficulty getting out of doors; six suicides (8 per cent) and five controls (10 per cent) had difficulty getting around the house; eight suicides (11 per cent) and 14 controls (9 per cent) had difficulty bathing; five suicides (7 per cent) and seven conrols (5 per cent) had difficulty dressing themselves; two suicides (3 per cent) and three controls (2 per cent) were either bedridden or chairbound; and ten suicides (13 per cent) compared with 19 controls (13 per cent) had two or more of these locomotor disabilities.

Nor did suicides differ from controls on measures of the frequency of disorders of senses or of communication. Three suicides (4 per cent) and six controls (4 per cent) were registered as blind or partially sighted; impaired hearing affected three suicides and one control; dysphasia affected two suicides and three controls.

These findings show that, on these measures, suicides do not have significantly more handicap than controls. Suicides do have more pain, which may be an expression of mood disorder, and there is the suggestion of an increased incidence of hearing disorder, which is also found in surveys of the mentally ill.

CONCLUSIONS

The importance of physical disease in contributing to suicide is modest in comparison to that of mental disease. Certain physical diseases have a stronger association with suicide than others, but the association is seldom direct, being mediated through mood disorder, alcohol abuse or social difficulties.

3

Epilepsy and Suicide

The excess mortality of epilepsy is caused principally by death in status epilepticus and by accidents, especially drowning, associated with fits. Progressive fatal brain disease responsible for the fits also accounts for some deaths. Suicide as a contributor to the excess mortality is mentioned in the standard texts on epilepsy and in the literature, but without substantial evidence.

Epilepsy might coexist with a mental disorder predisposing to suicide because the same cerebral pathology, for example neoplasm or injury, is responsible for both. In other cases a condition with a high suicide rate, for example alcoholism or drug abuse, is the cause of fits. Further, the anticonvulsant drugs used to control epilepsy may produce psychological and behavioural changes leading to suicide. And the stigma attached to epilepsy, which affects patients' own view of themselves and other people's conduct towards them, could cause mood changes which contribute to suicide. Interestingly, although there are good reasons why epileptics should have a high suicide rate, only the last-mentioned is an outcome of the fit.

Statistical evidence suggests that epileptics do have more than their share of suicide, for epileptics are some ten to twenty times more common among samples of suicides (Barraclough *et al.*, 1974; Chynoweth *et al.*, 1980), open verdict deaths (Holding and Barraclough, 1975), accidental deaths resembling suicide (Holding and Barraclough, 1977), and attempted suicides (Hawton, Fagg and Marsack, 1980) than in the general population. The fact that anticonvulsant drugs cause several deaths classified as suicide each year (Barraclough, 1974a) is in keeping with this conclusion.

The literature review showing that epilepsy has a high suicide rate, briefly mentioned in the previous chapter, will now be described, followed by an outline of a case study of 15 epileptics who killed themselves. The case study illustrates the importance of mental illness and of social factors, rather than the fits themselves, in the suicide of epileptics.

LITERATURE REVIEW ON THE SUICIDE RATE OF EPILEPSY

The literature search produced results which can be grouped under the following headings: temporal lobe epilepsy, institutionalised epileptics, outpatient epileptics and insurance statistics (Table 3.1). The results show, broadly speaking, that epilepsy has a raised suicide rate, and that the more severe the epilepsy the higher the rate becomes (Barraclough, 1987).

Four studies of the aftermath of temporal lobe epilepsy concur that the risk of suicide is greatly increased, perhaps by as much as 25 times. The surgically treated cases from Taylor and Marsh's (1977) series had the greatest risk, and those from Lindsay et al. (1979) had the least. Lindsay et al.'s cases approximate to an unselected sample, while Taylor and Marsh's would have been selected for surgery because of their marked severity.

Three studies of severely affected institutionalised patients with epilepsy all report an increased risk of suicide. White et al.'s (1979) finding, based on a fine study intended to assess whether anticonvulsant drugs cause cancer, shows the risk to be increased five times, similar to Prudhomme's (1941) result of nearly 50 years ago. Khron's (1963) method does not permit an expected rate to be calculated; however the high proportion of all deaths due to suicide in his sample is similar to that in White et al.

Eight papers describe follow-up studies of patients with epilepsy identified at general hospitals, mainly in special clinics for epilepsy. Four report suicide to be increased (Dalby, 1969; Henrikson et al., 1970; Sillanpaa, 1973; Zielinski, 1974), and three not (Martin, 1974; Hauser, et al., 1980; Sillanpaa, 1983). The eighth paper I included because there are references to it (Penning et al., 1969) in the epilepsy literature on suicide, even though a suicide rate cannot be calculated from the data given. The results suggest that epileptics referred to hospital clinics have an increased suicide risk. Hauser et al.'s result, based on the study of an unselected sample of epileptics, showed an

Table 3.1: Follow-up Studies of Patients with Epilepsy Reporting Mortality from Suicide

Reference	Country	No. of Suicides Observed	No. of Suicides Expected	No. of dead	Percentage of deaths from suicide	Sample size	Follow-up period (years)
Currie, Heathfield, Henson et al. (1972)	England	3	0.3[a]	54 (12)	5 (25)	493[c]	1–25
Stepien, Bidzinski and Mazurowski (1969)	Poland	2	0.03[a]	3 (2)	67 (100)	77	1–9
Taylor and Marsh (1977)	England	9	0.2	37	24	193	5–24
Lindsay, Ounstead and Richards (1979)	England	1	0.05[a]	9 (6)	11 (17)	100	12–29
Prudhomme (1941)	USA	8	1.7	1,100	0.7	several thousand	14
Khron (1963)	Norway	3	N/K	107 (36)	3 (9)	not given	10
White, McLean and Howland (1979)	England	21	3.9	636 (425)	3 (5)	1980	6–27
Dalby (1969)	Denmark	2	0.2[a]	10	20	346	4–16
Henriksen, Juul-Jenson and Lund (1970)	Denmark	21	7	104 (79)	20 (26)	2,673	25
Sillanpaa (1973)	Finland	1	0.001[a]	18	6	245	10
Sillanpaa (1983)	Finland	1	0.7[a]	29 (15)	3 (7)	245	21
Zielinski (1974)	Poland	16	2[b]	218	7	6,710	3
Hauser, Annegers and Elverback (1980)	USA	3	3	187	2	618	0–30+
Martin (1974)	Switzerland	0	0.2[a]	12	0	100	12–20
Penning, Muller and Clomps (1969)	Switzerland	4	N/K	171	2	202	N/K
Society of Actuaries (Impairment Study 1951) (1954)	USA	2	0.7	157	2	1,000	1–15

N/K = not known.
Figures in parentheses are deaths unrelated to epilepsy or its treatment.
[a] Expected number based on sample size and follow-up period applying national suicide rate.
[b] Calculated from author's statement that suicide was five times commoner in men and ten times commoner in women.
[c] Patients aged 15 and over from sample of 666.
Source: Barraclough (1987).

average suicide rate, which suggests the risk of suicide is related to severity of disease.

The Impairment Study 1951 (Society of Actuaries, 1954) followed 1,000 insured people with epilepsy in remission for up to 15 years. On the basis of two deaths and three policies, the Study concluded that insured epileptics had a risk of suicide approximately two and a half times greater than the healthy, or unimpaired, insured person. The chosen comparison group, unimpaired insured lives, does not permit a conclusion whether the risk of suicide for insured epileptics is above that of the general population.

These findings show epilepsy is associated with a greater risk of suicide than any other single physical condition. Temporal lobe epilepsy, severe epilepsy and epilepsy with handicap have a greatly increased risk, 25 times for temporal lobe epilepsy and five times for severe epilepsy. Epileptics referred to special clinics may also have an increased risk, by some four times in those studies reporting an excess of observed over expected deaths.

The cause of the increased risk cannot be ascertained from these studies. Two (Martin, 1974 and Currie *et al.*, 1972) mention alcohol. However in another study of the mortality of epilepsy, but one which did not consider cause of death separately, mental illness is given as the chief reason for an increase of two and a half times in the expected mortality of epileptics attending the neurological clinic of the Caroline Institute, Stockholm (Alstrom, 1950). Since the exact causes of death were not given, the relation between suicide and mental illness cannot be clarified.

A CLINICAL STUDY OF EPILEPTICS WHO COMMITTED SUICIDE

To explore the reasons why epileptics have an increased tendency to suicide, and to discover features which might assist in identifying the epileptic at high risk for suicide, we studied the clinical and social features of a series of epileptics who had killed themselves (Barraclough and Chynoweth, in press). A point of particular interest was the importance of the fits themselves in predisposing to suicide.

Because material of this kind is uncommon we felt justified in combining the epileptic subjects from two inquiries: the 100 suicides from Sussex, England (Barraclough, Bunch, Nelson and Sainsbury, 1974), and 125 suicides from Brisbane, Australia (Chynoweth, Tonge and Armstrong, 1980). Both inquiries used the method described in Chapter 1.

Epilepsy, for the purpose of this study, was defined as a history of fits in the year before death. Using this definition there were 15 epileptic suicides from the combined sample of 225 suicides, five from the English study and ten from the Australian, giving a prevalence of 67 per 1,000, some 16 times that in the general population, in which the prevalence of epilepsy is 4 per 1,000. Seven cases were men and eight were women; their ages ranged from 26 to 80 years.

The seizure type was grand mal in 14 cases and petit mal in one. No case had temporal lobe attacks — surprising in the light of the high suicide rate for this type of epilepsy indicated by the literature review. The cause of fits, a somewhat arbitrary judgement in some cases because of overuse of alcohol and barbiturate, was 'idiopathic' in five cases, alcoholism in three, barbiturate abuse in three, cerebral trauma in three, and cerebrovascular accident in one.

None had uncontrolled or disabling fits. None resided in an institution on account of epilepsy, although one lived in a mental hospital, having been admitted there 20 years before death with an 'epileptic psychosis'. In all but one case the history of fits was longer than a year, and in seven cases it was more than 10 years. Fits had begun in the teens in four cases and in adult life in eleven. Three were known to have experienced a fit shortly before the suicidal act. Ten of the 15 were prescribed regular anticonvulsant drugs, phenytoin for nine, phenobarbitone for four and primidone for one. Six cases had one anticonvulsant prescribed and four cases had two.

As for all suicides, contact with doctors was recent for most cases. Five had been seen in the week before death, five in the month and four in the year; the fifteenth, a doctor, treated herself. Two cases were outpatients of an epilepsy clinic, two were psychiatric inpatients and three more attended psychiatric outpatients.

Psychiatric diagnosis

Fourteen of the 15 were judged mentally ill, and the diagnoses made are listed in Table 3.2.

51

Table 3.2: Psychiatric Diagnosis of 15 Suicides with Epilepsy

Primary diagnosis	Secondary diagnosis	N
Depression	None	4
	Alcohol and barbiturate addiction	2
	Alcoholism	1
	Dementia and barbiturate addiction	1
	Barbiturate addiction	1
Anxiety neurosis	Alcoholism	2
Alcoholism	Dementia	1
Addiction	To barbiturates	1
	To glutethimide	1
Not mentally ill		1
		15

The primary diagnosis was depression in nine cases, and this was the only diagnosis in four. In the remaining five, depression was accompanied by alcoholism and barbiturate addiction (two), alcoholism (one), barbiturate addiction and dementia (one) and barbiturate addiction (one). Two cases were diagnosed anxiety neurosis with alcoholism, two addiction to barbiturate and one case was diagnosed alcoholism which had been severe and long-lasting enough to have resulted in alcoholic dementia.

Personality disorder using Schneider's criteria (Schneider, 1950) was diagnosed in four cases. All four were addicted to drugs.

Two cases were mentally handicapped as well as being mentally ill.

A past history of psychiatric treatment was present in eight cases. Ten were known to have attempted suicide before. Five had family histories of psychiatric treatment for parents, siblings or children.

This summary shows an exceptionally high prevalence of mental illness, addiction, mental handicap and personality disorder, far beyond that found among unselected samples of people with epilepsy. The mental disorder had an important handicapping effect, nine cases being significantly handicapped and five disabled by it.

The mental illness had usually been recognised, judging by the prescription of psychotropic drugs. At least one psychotropic drug had been prescribed for twelve cases, and for six cases two or more. Phenothiazines had been prescribed in four cases.

An antidepressant had been prescribed in one case — rather few considering the clinical evidence of mood disorder. No-one was having ECT.

There was good evidence that all 15 abused alcohol or prescribed drugs, and sometimes both — barbiturates being the most common. The scope of the drug prescription and drug taking, including alcohol, is a measure of attempts to control distress. Substance abuse on this scale must have undermined fit control, even when not the primary cause of fits.

Physical illness

Physical disease of some significance was present in eleven of the 15 cases, often associated with mental symptoms, and closely connected with the epilepsy in a most interesting way, as follows:

Alcohol caused both a physical disease and fits in three cases: post-gastrectomy dumping syndrome; alcoholic gastritis, peripheral neuritis and alcoholic dementia; fatty liver.

Vascular disease resulted in cerebral pathology and fits in two cases: cerebral infarct and dementia; cerebral infarct and congestive heart failure.

Barbiturate addiction was associated with possibly spurious illness and fits in two cases: recurrent pancreatitis (requiring three laparotomies to investigate, yet a normal abdomen at autopsy); multiple admissions for probable Munchausen syndrome.

Head injury caused both deafness and fits in one case.

Pregnancy, although not a disease state, does warrant mention in this context, because two previous pregnancies were associated with fits in one case.

Six cases had previously had major abdominal surgery. Five of these were women. It will be recalled that there were eight women in the sample. Two had laparotomies (one for an unknown reason, the other for recurring pancreatitis), two had cholecystectomies, and one a hysterectomy.

Disfiguring skin conditions affected two cases: whole-body psoriasis; extensive burn scars over the trunk.

Impaired exercise tolerance and energy, because of heart disease, affected two cases.

Social circumstances

Social factors are strongly related to suicide. We assessed domestic environment, work, and conflict with the law.

A stable home life is a strong influence in sustaining health and normal behaviour, and helping the ill to cope with the consequences of sickness. The home life of this sample of epileptics was either absent or unsatisfactory. Six had no conventional home life, four living by themselves and two living in non-private accommodation. Many who live alone do so by choice and prefer it, but this was not so here. All four did so unwillingly, for the following reasons: evicted from friend's house; housekeeper left; wife deserted; wife died. The fifth lived in lodgings with a mentally disturbed landlady after a recent discharge from a mental hospital, and the sixth resided in a mental hospital back ward with a move to a new ward pending. It is worth noting that the living circumstances for all these six were new, resulting in a need for adjustment.

Six shared a home with a spouse, but a home of misery, or disorder, or both, as demonstrated by the following summary of their circumstances: on leave from a mental hospital; incapable from dementia and barbiturate addiction; battering his wife (two cases); being battered by her husband (two cases).

Three lived with people other than spouses, none in normal circumstances, as the following list illustrates. One, who was pregnant, lived with her two pre-school-age children, her husband having deserted. The second lived with his father and two brothers, having been discharged from prison 2 weeks before his death. The third lived with her two adopted children, a friend and the friend's father, her husband having deserted.

None of these 15 lived in a 'normal' home, a private house comprising two or more related people, with a common housekeeping, living on good terms and in an orderly way. This finding is most striking and must differ remarkably from the circumstances of most epileptics living outside institutions.

Work

The satisfaction and psychological support of working life is an important component to mental well-being and to sustaining those who are sick, whatever the type of illness, but this was not so here. The sexes are described separately because their working lives differ.

Five of the seven men were of working age. One had a satisfactory working life but the other four did not, the reasons for this being as follows: unemployment following recent discharge from prison, failure as an author because of alcoholism, compulsory retirement because of alcoholism and then demotion in the new job, impending and unwanted retirement. Of the two over retirement age, one had nothing to do, the other seemed content with an institutional life in a mental hospital. Only two of the seven therefore had satisfactory work or retirement.

Five of the eight women were housewives and four could not manage their homes because of frequent episodes of barbiturate intoxication. The fifth coped under strain. Two other women were invalid pensioners and neither could manage their home or affairs because of sedative addiction and mental illness. The eighth woman was employed, having resumed general medical practice after a year's voluntary suspension because of barbiturate addiction.

Taking the sexes together, employment was normal for one only of the six people of working age, and domestic work for one woman of the seven at home, a striking deviation from customary experience.

Unlawful conduct

Unlawful conduct can be a sign of mental illness, or personality disorder, and usually results in distress for offender, victim and near relatives. Unlawful behaviour was a source of distress for eight epileptic suicides, as the offender for six and as the victim for two. The offences in question were: persistent theft resulting in a prison sentence; debt; driving under the influence of alcohol; driving under the influence of sedatives and attending patients under the influence of drugs; wife beating (two cases); and being beaten by husband (two cases).

Comparison with non-epileptic suicides

If epilepsy plays an important part in causing suicide, epileptic

55

Table 3.3: Suicides With and Without Epilepsy Compared on Presence of Physical Disease

Case	Epileptic suicides (N = 15)	Common factor between epilepsy and physical disease	Non-epileptic suicides (N = 30)
3	Pregnant	Pregnancy caused epilepsy	
	Whole-body psoriasis		
5	Infarct right basal ganglia	Cerebral vascular disease	Prostatic cancer
	Dementia		
6	Post-gastrectomy dumping syndrome	Alcohol	
7	Alcohol dementia	Alcohol	
8	Hypertensive heart disease		Cushing's syndrome
	Fatty liver (alcoholic)	Alcohol	Fractured left maxilla
10	Cerebral atrophy	Repeated blows to the head	Active pulmonary tuberculosis
11	Recurrent oedema and weight gain (possibly spurious)	Personality disorder leading to barbiturate addiction	
12	60% bilateral deafness Chronic otitis media	Head injury	Stomach cancer Multiple infarcts, occipital cortex
14	Recurrent pancreatitis (possibly spurious)	Personality disorder leading to drug addiction	Left hemiplegia
15	Congestive heart failure Cyst left frontal lobe	Vascular disease	Partially blind Glaucoma
	No significant disease 5 (33%)		24 (80%)

suicides should differ from non-epileptic suicides in ways related to the tendency to fit. To test for this possibility the 15 epileptic suicides were compared with an age/sex-matched sample of 30, selected by a random method from the 210 suicides without epilepsy in the same study samples.

The two groups are equivalent demographically, and on

measures of mental illness, social isolation and social stress. They differ on the frequency of significant physical disease diagnosed before death, or discovered after death as a result of the autopsy (Table 3.3). Furthermore, a link between the physical disease and the epilepsy is clear in ten of the epileptic suicides.

CONCLUSIONS

Epilepsy is associated with a high suicide rate. The link is probably an indirect one, in cases where cerebral pathology or drug and alcohol abuse is responsible for both mood disorder and fits. Our case study showed that fits alone are not an important contributor to suicide, for the following reasons. Epileptic suicides closely resemble other suicides in their depressive psychopathology, abuse of alcohol and drugs, poor interpersonal relationships, and socially disrupted lives. Their epilepsy had usually been long-standing and was under reasonable control, few subjects having had fits in the period immediately preceding death. The fits themselves seemed to be of minor importance in comparison with mental illness, physical illness, drug and alcohol abuse, personality disorder, and social disorganisation, which were evident in all cases. In these ways the epileptic suicides resemble suicides without epilepsy.

The person with epilepsy, but otherwise of sound mental health and stable social circumstances, probably has no more than an average risk of suicide.

To flesh out these findings four case histories from the 15 are here summarised. The histories demonstrate the relative unimportance of fits as a handicap compared to mental illness, addiction and social disorder.

An unemployed, unmarried fisherman was 26 when he committed suicide with an overdose of barbiturates. He had come out of prison 2 weeks before to live with his father and brother, both alcoholics.

He was born into a fishing family, the second of seven children. Because of low intelligence and truancy he had little education. His mother died when he was 13. Heavy drinking and barbiturate abuse started soon afterwards.

A criminal record began at 17. By the time of death there were convictions for breaking and entering, stealing, common assault, dangerous driving, unlawful use of a motor vehicle, drunkenness, resisting arrest, and breach of probation.

Recurring episodes of disturbed conduct resulted in six admissions to psychiatric hospitals with the diagnosis of psychopathy and depression. His self-confidence was impaired by disfiguring burns sustained in a fishing boat explosion 4 years before death. On several occasions he had said his life was not worth living, and had attempted suicide twice before the fatal overdose. On the day he died he told his brother he meant to kill himself.

Grand mal epilepsy developed at 18 years, the cause unknown. In spite of taking phenytoin the fits continued, although not frequently enough to be a serious handicap. At the time of death thioridazine, sodium amylobarbitone, and chloral hydrate were also prescribed.

A 51-year-old widow killed herself with an overdose of glutethimide. She had been discharged from a psychiatric hospital 4 months before, and was boarding with a 71-year-old landlady who had dementia.

One of five children, she was brought up in a strict home. From early childhood her behaviour was disturbed, stealing from parents and truanting from school.

After school she spent 18 months in the army, then worked as a maid, marrying at 23, her husband being much older. Their only child was treated for depression and attempted suicide as an adult. This family history was extended by a sister also treated for depression.

Drug abuse and depression began when she was 38. A suicide attempt when she was 41 resulted in hospital admission and ECT for depression. When her elderly husband died she was, at 45, left to live alone, socially isolated. Repeated admissions to mental hospitals followed, with diagnoses of drug abuse, personality disorder, depression, and on one occasion paranoid schizophrenia.

Grand mal epilepsy attributed to drug abuse began 10 years before death. She was prescribed phenytoin, trifluoperazine, diazepam, and nitrazepam, and obtained other sedatives from different doctors, glutethimide being preferred.

A 55-year-old butcher was living alone when he killed himself with carbon monoxide gas. His wife had left him for another man 10 days earlier. He believed she had gone for good, though she planned to return.

Nothing was known of his early life. When 27 a car accident resulted in a skull fracture which left him 60 per cent deaf. The petit mal epilepsy which developed shortly afterwards was attributed to the accident. The epilepsy caused occasional 'blackouts', not troublesome and not treated. For many years he had abused alcohol. His liver was enlarged (2415 g) at postmortem.

After his wife left, symptoms of a depressive illness developed and he told his son-in-law that he felt he would be better off dead.

A 41-year-old married woman killed herself with an overdose of alcohol and barbiturates.

For 6 years her unhappy marriage was made worse by repeated batterings from her husband including two stabbings. Nineteen hospital attendances and seven admissions were required to treat the injuries. Low intelligence, poor education and a dependent nature prevented her leaving a violent man.

In 10 years many admissions to mental hospitals had diagnosed 'a pathologically dependent personality with an anxiety state' and described addiction to alcohol, barbiturates and pethidine. Six admissions to general hospitals, resulting in three laparotomies, were required for episodes of abdominal pain attributed to recurring pancreatitis.

Grand mal fits thought to result from brain damage sustained during a severe assault by the husband began 6 years before death. Phenytoin partly controlled the convulsions, which were not frequent.

Postmortem failed to find evidence of pancreatitis, suggesting some other cause for the abdominal pain.

4

Social Relations of Suicide

This chapter will consider the relation to suicide of a number of human experiences which for convenience are subsumed under the term 'social'. To Durkheim, social influences were paramount in causing suicide, and he devoted his book *Le Suicide* to demonstrating this fact.

Behavioural scientists after Durkheim have continued this style of inquiry, which relies in the main on data collected in the course of public administration. Not having to collect the raw data is an attraction of this economical approach. The results of these inquiries describe the association between two or more measurements made on populations as large as a nation, as small as a city and even smaller. Strictly speaking the results are true only of the population, and cannot be applied to the individuals who make up the population. This has not prevented explanations of conditions predisposing to suicide at the individual level being derived from these results which, being at such a distance from the phenomena to be explained, are susceptible of error of interpretation. The correct approach to explaining suicide at this level, to study a large enough series of cases in a controlled way, was used by Sainsbury (1955) in his inquiry into the social relations of suicide in London. Using this case study approach, the relation of suicide and some social variables can be examined directly. Further, the interaction between one social variable and another can be assessed, and the influence of ill-health studied. The social conditions associated with suicide can be produced by mental illness, and these social conditions may alter the response to otherwise tolerable illness. The aggregation of suicides in decaying city centres, for instance, may result from the migration of the mentally ill, who are at high risk of suicide, to such areas, where the social conditions further increase their suicide risk.

The social phenomena considered in this chapter are circumstances and events which can be defined and measured, for all cases, in the absence of the chief witness. This handicap limits the range of testable hypotheses. For example the conversations which a suicide had with friends in the week before death would provide a test of a 'social isolation' hypothesis, the suicide being predicted to have fewer and less satisfactory contacts than a control. But because of the subjective element in the definition of 'friend' the definition cannot be applied when the subject is absent. Nor can the people talked to by the impending suicide be discovered without inquiries so large as to be impractical. A more modest approach to test such a social isolation hypothesis is to find the number of contacts with first-degree relatives in the week before death. First-degree relatives, objectively defined by formal tie, talk with each other enough for one or two key figures to know the facts the researcher wants. This explanation gives some idea of our approach.

Each section in the following account describes an attempt to test a 'social' hypothesis. The hypotheses are tested by comparing observations made on the suicides and the controls from the clinical study described in Chapter 1, and by using data from the Census for England and Wales.

BEREAVEMENT

Events which result in loss are commonly believed to cause people to kill themselves. Records of inquests from the time of Henry VII contain accounts of suicide following tragic events, as do those of today. The most severe are the deaths of near relatives, especially husband or wife, parents, brothers and sisters, and children. Death of a parent is the commonest, being a natural consequence of increasing age. That virtually everyone survives the experience of loss events without committing suicide does not prevent virtually everyone 'understanding' the suicide which follows a tragedy.

If bereavement and suicide are related, suicides should have more bereavements than would be expected by chance. Suicide is well suited to testing bereavement hypotheses scientifically because death, both independent and dependent variable, is

61

definable and dateable with precision. Our material permitted the testing of hypotheses about the relationship between suicide and parental death.

Accuracy of remembered dates of death

Bereavement studies which have correlated mental illness with recent or past parental death have relied on the subject's memory for ascertaining parent death dates. Such dates can be wrong because of faulty recollection, deliberate misinformation to conceal something considered shameful, such as illegitimacy, or guessing by people who do not know. The temptation of the interviewer to 'help' may also contribute.

Because of the difficulty we found in discovering the date of parental death from near relatives of suicides, we checked their information with the date on the death entry at the General Register Office. Error was common, and this influenced us to study the accuracy with which the dates of parental death are remembered, an inquiry not previously undertaken.

The accuracy with which the dates of parental deaths are remembered was measured for the group of 150 control subjects described in Chapter 1, an older group than the general population, and containing an over-representation of men, single, widowed and divorced. We compared the date of the parental death given by the control subject with the date on the death entry at the General Register Office, the Death Register being searched for 5 years on either side of the remembered date before abandoning the search (Barraclough and Bunch, 1973).

The 150 subjects had 208 dead parents — 101 mothers and 107 fathers. We traced death entries for 179 (86 per cent) of them (Table 4.1). Thirteen death entries were not searched for because parents had died abroad, in the Armed Forces or because of insufficient information. Faults in the Death Register, misinformation to conceal illegitimacy, and memory being out by more than 10 years accounted for the other 16 cases.

Eleven per cent of subjects were 3 years or more in error, 20 per cent were 2 or more years out, and 40 per cent 1 year or more. Error was equal for both mother and father deaths. The longer the period since the death the greater the inaccuracy. Of deaths occurring more than 20 years in the past, nearly half the remembered dates were wrong.

Table 4.1: Date of Parent Death: Time since death and memory error

Time since death*	Years in error of recollection							
	Correct		1–2 years		⩾ 3 years		Total	
	N	%	N	%	N	%	N	%
< 5 years	14	78	4	22	0	0	18	100
5–9 years	42	62	18	26	8	12	68	100
> 10 years	52	56	29	31	12	13	93	100
All	108	60	51	28	20	11	179	100

* From death certificates.

The absence of bias to over or underestimate the period since death means the estimate of the mean period since parent deaths using remembered dates will not differ from the truëmean. The memory error term is a random normal variate which sums to zero. But the error term inflates the variance especially for long-ago deaths, tending to obscure real differences between the means of study groups and their controls. This effect will be greatest for studies of parent death in childhood using small samples, and may account for the inconsistent findings of published inquiries on this topic.

The errors were minimum ones based on the death certificates found. The 16 parental deaths with undiscovered certificates probably occurred outside the 10-year range searched. With their inclusion, the proportion of correct ratings drops from 60 per cent to 55 per cent.

This result demonstrates that recollected dates of parental death are inaccurate and should not be used in scientific inquiries if unsupported by documents. The inaccuracy probably inflates the proportion of father deaths in childhood because illegitimacy may be recorded as death. Our own findings are affected by memory error, for 15 per cent of parental deaths of suicide and control groups could not be discovered in the Death Register.

Early parental bereavement

Death of a parent during childhood has been reported to predispose to mental illness, delinquency, attempted suicide

63

and suicide in adult life. Evidence for this effect is conflicting, perhaps because most studies rely on the subject's own memory of the date of parental death. One study, which did not rely on memory after the event, found that 225 college students who subsequently committed suicide had been bereaved of their fathers at the time of their entry to college more often than 450 control students (Paffenbarger and Asnes, 1965). By using data from documents completed many years before the suicide occurred, the inquiry avoided memory error. However the finding may not apply to suicide in the general population, since US college students are a special group.

We tested the hypothesis that suicides more often lose a parent by death before reaching the age of 16 than does the general population (Bunch, Barraclough, Nelson and Sainsbury, 1971b). The samples comprised 75 of the suicides and the 150 controls described in Chapter 1. The death dates of parents, collected during interviews with relatives for the suicides, or the controls themselves, were checked against the Death Register as described in the previous section.

Seventeen per cent of suicides compared with 19 per cent of controls had lost a parent by death before reaching the age of 16, a difference not statistically significant. There were no significant differences in the proportions of suicides and controls bereaved of a mother, a father or of either parent (Table 4.2). The result is not materially affected by confining the inquiry to deaths confirmed by death entry: 14 per cent of suicides and 13 per cent of controls lost a parent whose death certificate was traced.

The influence might relate more to suicide in the severely mentally ill. Eighteen per cent (seven) of the 39 suicides having psychiatric treatment at the time they died, or who had had psychiatric treatment in the past, were bereaved of a parent before the age of 16, compared with 16 per cent (six) of the other 36 suicides.

The bereavements of suicides with histories of attempted suicide and those without such histories were also similar.

Although a small sample, this material was consecutive, the control group carefully selected and the death dates verified in over 80 per cent of cases. If parent bereavement in childhood were an important factor for adult suicide, in England, this inquiry ought to have shown some trend pointing in that direction.

Table 4.2: Death of a Parent before Subject was 16

Age	Suicide (N = 75)		Control (N = 150)	
(years)	N	%	N	%
0–4	5	7	8	5
5–9	5	7	12	8
10–15	3	4	8	5
0–15	13	17	28	19

Recent parental death

In contrast to the influence of early parental death on adult mental health, the effect of recent parental death has received little attention. Since the death of a parent is an event which every adult expects to experience, and since common observation shows this event is usually survived without undue or prolonged distress, and even sometimes with relief, this is not so surprising. However, during interviews with relatives of suicides we observed a number of instances where suicide followed a parental death. Some relatives remarked about adverse changes in mood, behaviour and social life resulting from the bereavement, which they believed caused the suicide. This experience led us to make a statistical and case study inquiry about the relation between recent parental death and suicide, using the clinical and social observations made on the 75 suicides comparing their experience with that of the 150 controls (Bunch et al., 1971a).

We defined recent parental death as occurring within 5 years of the suicide or of the control interview. McMahon and Pugh's (1965) study of suicide following widowhood showed 5 years accounted for most of the excess mortality from suicide attributable to spouse death. The effects of parent death which we observed in the suicides seemed similar to those of widowing.

Similar proportions of suicides and of controls had lost a parent by death at the inception of the 5-year period, a finding consistent with that of the previous section on parental death in childhood, indicating the suicide group to be typical of the general population in this respect.

Within the 5 years leading to the day of the suicide, or of the control interview (for convenience the inception period and the index day), four fathers of suicides and five fathers of controls died, 22 per cent and 11 per cent respectively of those at risk. The difference, although not statistically significant, is in the expected direction. Mother-bereavement was, however, significantly greater for suicides. Sixteen suicides, 50 per cent of those at risk, lost a mother during the inception period compared with 12 controls, 20 per cent of those at risk (Table 4.3). The greatest difference between suicides and controls occurred during the 3 years before the suicide for both mother death and loss of either parent.

Table 4.3: Death of a Parent in Past 5 Years

	Father		Mother	
Suicide	4/18	(22%)	16/32	(50%)
Control	5/45	(11%)	12/61	(20%)

The loss of both parents by three suicides (17 per cent) and one control (2 per cent) in the inception period, although not statistically significant, must on common-sense grounds add weight to the observation that suicide is preceded by an excess of bereavement.

Since the controls may have been an aberrantly healthy, or unhealthy, group we compared the observed mortality of the parents of suicides and the parents of controls for the inception period with an expected mortality calculated from Life Tables. The findings corroborated those of the previous paragraph.

Bereavement studies have suggested that older age and male sex predispose to mental illness following spouse death. We compared the suicides with the controls to see whether a similar effect applied for parental death, taking account of the sex of the parent and marital status, since observations during interviewing had suggested mother deaths might be more damaging, and that being unmarried increased vulnerability.

Eleven (28 per cent) of the 40 male suicides had lost a mother in the inception period compared to eight (10 per cent) of the 80 male controls, a significant difference. These eleven suicides are 52 per cent of the 21 male suicides with a mother alive at the beginning of the inception period, compared with the controls where the eight are 22 per cent of the 37 with mothers alive at the outset of the inception period. Of the single, widowed or divorced males with mothers alive at the beginning of the inception period, eight (62 per cent) of the 13 suicides lost a mother compared to one (7 per cent) of the 15 controls. Of the married, three (37 per cent) of the eight suicides and seven (32 per cent) of the 22 controls lost a mother. The relationship was greatest for the older single male, all three of whom with mothers alive at the beginning of the inception period were bereaved of their mothers before they killed themselves.

Five (14 per cent) of the 35 female suicides lost a mother in the inception period compared to four (6 per cent) of the 70 controls. Although in the expected direction this difference was not statistically significant and the analysis not pursued.

Three (8 per cent) of the 40 male suicides lost a father compared to four (5 per cent) of the 80 male controls. One (3 per cent) of the 35 female suicides lost a father compared to one (1 per cent) of the 70 female controls.

The statistical analysis supported the clinical impression and showed, for unmarried men only, a strong relationship between death of their mother and subsequent suicide.

Previous mental illness, especially depression, is known to increase the risk of abnormal bereavement reactions. We looked at our material to see if this were true of suicide. A history of psychiatric treatment or attempted suicide before the bereavement, or a history of psychiatric treatment for a first-degree family member, was present for ten of the 17 bereaved suicides compared with only one of the 16 bereaved controls. A loading for 'proneness to mental illness' therefore distinguishes those bereaved people who subsequently kill themselves. In seven of the ten cases the illness was depression, in two drug addiction and in one schizophrenia.

Since social circumstances are so strongly related to suicide we compared suicides with controls to determine if loss of a parent had resulted in social changes which might increase risk for suicide. These changes were: being left living alone, financial loss, moving house, loss of a social relationship, other persisting social changes. Four of the 17 suicides bereaved of either parent had to live alone as a result, compared to one of the 16 bereaved controls, a difference in the expected direction although without statistical significance. In other respects the

67

controls did not differ remarkably from the suicides.

The absence of a measurable association between suicide and social changes following parental bereavement suggests that bereavement encourages suicide by an influence on personality, and by increasing vulnerability to mental illness. The group most sensitive to this effect are unmarried men, of any age, bereaved of a mother.

The different responses to bereavement of suicides and controls are striking. Two suicide case summaries illustrate the remarkable changes which followed death of a mother:

A single man of 51 had lived in the same lodgings, and held the same job, for 10 years. His health had always been good. Although he did not live with her, his mother was his chief confidante. After she died he became mentally ill, was treated in two hospitals for anxiety neurosis and agitated depression, and made several suicide attempts. During the 2 years which followed the bereavement he had five residences, the last living with a sister. Stable employment disappeared and he had seven jobs. He hanged himself during the lunch break in his last job.

A single woman of 66 had an exceptionally close relationship with her mother. They were described as 'like sisters' and had always lived together, sharing the same bedroom. For 40 years they worked in the same factory, went out together, and took holidays together. After the mother died the daughter deteriorated in health, complaining of poor sleep and appetite. A year after the bereavement she was retired from work, because of repeated absence without cause, and 'letting herself go'. She continued to live in her mother's house, with a single brother whom she disliked, for 4 years after her mother's death. Then she committed suicide by coal gas poisoning.

ANNIVERSARIES

The psychiatric literature, especially that written from the psychoanalytic viewpoint, is replete with references to anniversaries of bereavements precipitating depression and suicide. Zilboorg (1937) suggested suicides take their lives on the anniversary of their parent's death to expiate their guilt for having caused the death through an unconscious wish. Others have interpreted suicide as an attempt at a rebirth or a new beginning with the lost love object, instancing the anniversary effect in support. The absence, at the time of their writing, of an established statistical association between suicide and anniversaries did not deter psychoanalytically oriented writers from accepting that an association exists. Clinical experience and an intriguing theory justified the belief.

An inquiry which established an association between spouse bereavement and suicide in the 4 years following the spouse's death, using hundreds of cases, also looked at the anniversary effect by testing for an excess number of suicides in the week on either side of the anniversary of the spouse's death. None was found. The authors concluded the effect of the anniversary of a spouse's death on predisposition to suicide, if it exists at all, must be weak (McMahon and Pugh, 1965).

That suicide might be associated with bereavement anniversaries of another kind was pointed out by relatives of suicides we interviewed who mentioned, without prompting, instances of suicide occurring close to the anniversary of the death of a parent.

To test for a statistical association between the date of the suicide and the anniversary of a parent death we used a sample of 65 suicides which occurred over a calendar year, taken from the population of 75 suicides previously described. We chose a year of deaths to avoid bias from the different seasonal variations in mortality from suicide and from natural death.

The simplest way of calculating the expected frequency is to assume each time interval has an equal chance of occurring in each case. There are then 61/365 chances of a death occurring within 30 days of a birthday or on the birthday itself. One-sixth of deaths would by chance occur within 30 days of a birthday.

Fifty-two (80 per cent) of the 65 suicides had parents who died in England and Wales, with one or both parental death certificates traced. This gave documented as opposed to recollected parental death dates, which would be the best estimate of the date remembered by the suicide.

Of the 52 suicides, 17 occurred within 30 days of a parent's anniversary, and four occurred within 30 days of both parents' death anniversaries. The difference between observed and expected numbers of suicides for this period was statistically significant for father's anniversaries but not mother's (Table 4.4). Thirteen suicides occurred in the 30 days before and after a father death anniversary compared with 6.8 expected. The four double anniversaries, all female suicides, were also greater than would be expected. We concluded that the anniversary of a father death, and a double anniversary of both parents dying, increases risk of a suicide (Bunch and Barraclough, 1971).

Table 4.4: Suicide in Relation to Anniversaries of Parental Death

Days from anniversary of death	Mother death		Father death	
	Observed	Expected	Observed	Expected
0–30	8	7	13	6.8
31–182	34	35	28	34.2
		NS		$p = 0.01$

Expected calculated by assuming the probability of a suicide occurring in the anniversary period is 61/365.

What factors distinguish the anniversary from the non-anniversary suicide? The length of time since the parent's death, age, parent's age, and marital status did not distinguish the two groups. But, significantly, daughters were more likely than sons to kill themselves in relation to their parent's death anniversary. This finding makes sense in view of the common observation that women recall anniversaries rather better than do men, and consider them more meaningful.

The finding, in this small sample, of a more than slight association between suicide date and parent death anniversary lends support to the long-held view of anniversaries precipitating some mental disturbance leading to suicide. The association with double anniversaries provides corroborative evidence.

Most of the suicides had been mentally ill, often for years, before they died, but had survived many previous anniversaries. More than 20 years separated parental death and suicide on average. If anniversaries influence the date selected for suicide, rather than causing the illness which determines the suicide, there must be other influences at work, and their nature is unknown.

BIRTHDAYS

Birthdays, another kind of anniversary, have been proposed as being associated with the date of death by Alderson (1975). He claimed to find an excess of deaths, from all causes, among those aged over 75, in the 3 months following their birthday. This finding, since proved to be an unexpected statistical artefact, prompted us to look for a birthday effect for suicide. An association with date of birth seems inherently more likely for self-inflicted death than for deaths from natural causes. A non-specific lowering of resistance to all disease would have to be invoked to explain a birthday influence of the kind Alderson observed. In contrast a birthday can be understood as likely to provoke unpleasant psychological experiences in the very old, determining the date of the suicide in a predisposed person. The parallel with parental death anniversaries is clear.

Developing this line of thought, we predicted that more elderly suicides than expected would die within 30 days of their birth date. The statistical model for calculating the expected number is the same as used for the parental death anniversaries described in the previous section.

The sample examined comprised 239 suicides and 43 undetermined deaths occurring in West Sussex and Portsmouth between 1961 and 1968. We included undetermined deaths because of their resemblance to suicide. The birth dates and the death dates came from inquest documents or personal interview with relations for 164 deaths, and from death certificates for 118.

Of the 35 deaths in persons aged 75 and more, eleven occurred within 30 days of a birthday, a statistically significant deviation from the expected number of just under six. For those aged 74 years and under, observed and expected numbers did not differ significantly (Table 4.5).

The birthday effect cases did not differ in sex, social class or mode of death from the other cases, but they were more likely to be living alone and not to be confused. A birthday probably exaggerates the loneliness of the oriented elderly depressive, so enhancing the risk of suicide in someone already predisposed (Barraclough and Shepherd, 1976a).

Table 4.5: Suicide in Relation to Suicide's Birthday

Days from birthday	74 and under		75 and over	
	Observed	Expected	Observed	Expected
0–30	45	41	11	5.8
31–182	202	206	24	29.2
	NS		$p = 0.02$	

TIMING OF SUICIDE ACT

The time rhythms of suicide have attracted inquiry since suicide statistics first became available in the early nineteenth century, and so are the subject of a large literature (Dublin, 1963). The time of day chosen for suicide has received least attention because of the difficulty of obtaining accurate information. Daily rhythms, the contrast of day and night, the influence of sleeping and waking, which profoundly affect human biology and social life, seem likely to exert some influence on the time of day suicide occurs. The time of the act leading to death, rather than the time of death itself, which can be considerably later, especially in poisoning cases, is worth study for this reason.

Durkheim's book contains statistical information giving numbers of suicides in each hour of the 24 for thousands of deaths. The validity of the information is not discussed. He concluded, in characteristic vein: 'Thus everything proves that if daytime is the part of the 24 hours most favourable to suicide it is because it is also the time when social life is at its height' (Durkheim, 1897). Morselli wrote similarly of the social influence, and introduced the impact of noise: 'The daily distribution of suicides is parallel to activity in business, to occupation and work, in short with the noise which characterises the life of modern society and not with quiet and observation' (Morselli, 1881, pp. 77–9).

Nothing of importance has been added to knowledge about hourly variation since Durkheim. Contemporary workers do not have the large sample statistics, sometimes for thousands of cases, with apparently accurately timed deaths, which the administrative machines of nineteenth-century Europe produced.

We decided to take a fresh look at hourly variation of time chosen for suicide using information collected on the 100 suicides described in Chapter 1. We attempted to time the start of the act which ended in death, by assessing the evidence of witnesses who had seen the suicide shortly before death, and the pathologist's opinion (Barraclough, 1976a).

Defining the time the act began to within an hour proved impossible for most cases. Instead we established for each case an interval during which the act must have begun. Three histories illustrate the method, and the difficulty of timing:

The suicide, who lived alone so there were no witnesses, poisoned himself with barbiturates, timing his note 0200 hours. Trusting the truthfulness of a man in such circumstances, the act was timed to precisely 0200 hours.

The suicide hanged himself at work. He was seen alive at 1200 hours and the body found at 1400 hours. The act was timed as occurring within a 2-hour interval.

The suicide lived alone and was last seen alive at 1600 hours on the 19th of the month. Her body was found at 2100 hours on the 26th. Because the pathologist timed the death between the 19th and the 23rd, and her brother called without getting an answer on the 20th at 1800 hours, the act of swallowing poison was timed as occurring in the 25-hour interval between 1700 hours on the 19th and 1800 hours on the 20th.

Using this approach 52 of the 100 suicides could be timed to an interval of less than 6 hours, a very low figure, and only 24 to an interval of 1 hour or less (Fig. 4.1). The inaccuracy was greatest for those living alone, and for those who died by poisoning, and least for those living with others and who died using a violent method such as hanging or shooting.

Because of the difficulty of analysing by hour of occurrence, cases were allocated to the quarter of the day when their suicide act began. Fifty-two cases could be so classified. Using this broader classification, fewer suicides occurred between midnight and 0600 hours, but not significantly fewer.

We concluded that any daily variation present could not be discovered using the case study approach. This finding places a question mark over the validity of the nineteenth-century

Figure 4.1: Distribution of Estimates of Time Period During Which Suicidal Action Began.

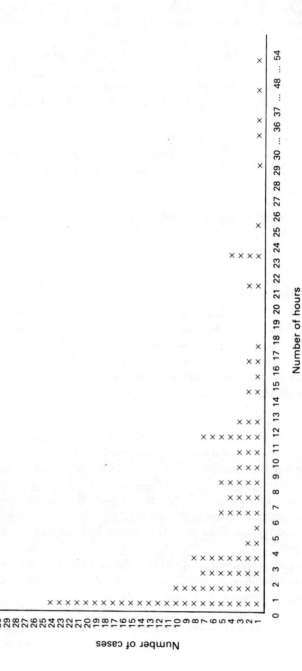

Reproduced with permission of Cambridge University Press, from Barraclough (1976a) 'Time of day chosen for suicide', *Psychological Medicine, 6*, 303–5

findings on daily rhythms for suicide. However since in those times fewer people lived alone and more suicides used violent methods, timing may have been easier.

The difficulty of timing suicides exactly must affect the interpretation of biochemical observations on suicide's brains.

UNEMPLOYMENT

The strongest protection against suicide, in Durkheim's opinion, was belonging to an organised work force, decentralised to avoid impersonality and to concentrate social energies, but linked to ensure a large-scale division of labour. The modern industrial state bears some resemblance to this model, at least for men, although not in the idealised way which Durkheim appears to have wished for.

Epidemiological studies

The scientific study of the relation between employment and suicide has used both the epidemiological and case study approaches. The epidemiological approach, by examining the relation between the rates of suicide and of employment, has shown a sharp increase in suicide at times of economic depression, and possibly a decrease in times of prosperity. The effect of prosperity has not received the same attention as the influence of economic depression. The association is most striking in the years of the great depression of the thirties when all industrial nations showed increases in their suicide rates, particularly for men in the middle and older age groups, suggesting this group to be most affected by employment loss. Alienation and social rejection may affect those who lose their jobs. This has not been proved by case studies of those who are thrown out of work and then kill themselves. However, case studies of men thrown out of work during an economic downturn, and remaining unemployed for no other reason than absence of opportunity, show high levels of depressive symptoms, suggesting that mood disorder may be one link between job loss and suicide (Melville, Hope, Bennison and Barraclough, 1985). Economic change may have less direct effects on the individual than job loss or gain, by an influence on morale and on social behaviour, changing the level of risk for suicide of a population through influences comparable to those exerted by war.

Case studies

The epidemiological approach draws attention to the apparent effect of a change in the rate of employment on the suicide rate of a population. To look at the relationship between employment and suicide for the individual requires the case study approach. In contrast to the many correlation studies of rates of suicide and employment, case studies are few, possibly because one is done with published official statistics, from an office chair, the other requires the labour of data collection.

The case study approach allows the work history to be looked at in depth and the interaction between work and other factors, particularly illness, to be examined. However the case study approach cannot examine the effects of large-scale changes in employment unless conducted over a lengthy period covering a time of economic change. None have done this; all are cross-sectional.

Case studies agree that the rate of unemployment among suicides is higher than for the general population, even at times of full employment. The postulated causes of the relation are, broadly speaking, the psychological, social and economic effects of unemployment, and the influence of mental illness, including alcoholism, in bringing about job loss. The weight given to each varies according to the method of inquiry and the theoretical outlook of the author.

Work histories of 75 suicides

Our inquiry into the relation between work and suicide used observations about the 75 suicides in our clinical study, and evaluated the findings using the control group of 150 people. The control group comprised a random sample of the general population of the same sex, age and marital status composition as the suicides, but not matched for social class or occupation. At the time of the inquiry full employment prevailed in the area. This inquiry resulted in a closer look at the work histories of a consecutive series of suicides than has been published elsewhere (Shepherd and Barraclough, 1980).

We hypothesised that compared to controls, the suicide sample would have:

fewer economically active,
less employment among the economically active,
more sick leave from work among the economically active,
more frequent changes of job among the economically active,
more early retirement,
more occupations with known high suicide rates.

The economically active

The occupational status of suicides on the day of their death, and controls on the day of their interview, showed 52 per cent of the 75 suicides to be economically active and 48 per cent inactive, using official definitions of economic activity, which approximate to being in the labour market or not (Table 4.6). The percentages for the 150 controls, 57 per cent and 43 per cent, show a trend in the predicted direction of more suicides being economically inactive. Four suicides of working age whose incurable mental illnesses kept them in hospital, and therefore out of the labour market, are responsible for the difference. The case history of schizophrenia in Chapter 1 illustrates how this can happen.

Within the economically active group, suicides and controls differed in two respects. Forty-nine per cent (19) of the 39 economically active suicides were in full-time paid employment compared to 80 per cent (67) of the 84 controls. The difference is accounted for by nine suicides who were unemployed (23 per cent) and six who were off sick (15 per cent), for which the control figures are 0 per cent and 5 per cent. Mental illness appeared to cause this high proportion of suicides, 15 of 39, who were not in full-time paid employment although in the labour market. Two of the nine unemployed suicides had been sacked because of alcoholism, and seven had given up their jobs because mental illness prevented them from coping at work. All the six suicides off sick had mental, not physical, disorders.

77

Table 4.6: Economic Status of Suicides and Controls

	Economically active			Economically inactive	
	In work	Off sick	Unemployed	Retired	Other
Suicides	24 (32%)	6 (8%)	9 (12%)	14 (19%)	22 (29%)
(*N*= 75)	[62%]	[15%]	[23%]	[39%]	[61%]
Controls	80 (54%)	4 (3%)	0 (0%)	24 (16%)	42 (27%)
(*N* = 150)	[95]	[5%]	[0%]	[36%]	[64%]

Percentages in square brackets are based on sub-totals for economically
active and economically inactive.

A case history illustrates how work may be abandoned under
the impact of mental illness.

A 23-year-old single man killed himself with carbon monoxide
gas by running a hose from the exhaust pipe into his car,
parked in a layby off a city bypass. Witnesses recalled him
being from the age of 6 an unhappy, hypersensitive child and
adolescent, irritable and disorganised and without friends.
He was self-conscious about his appearance and thought
people believed his walk peculiar. Periodically his misery
worsened. At 12 he swallowed iodine, saying he wanted to
die. At 15 he truanted from school for some weeks, again
saying he wished he were dead. When 14 and 16 he ran away
from home to London and then to Southampton, looking for
employment on a ship, because of unhappiness at school and
home.

When his full-time education stopped, at 16, he found
work in the printing trade. At 17 he stopped work and stayed
in bed. His mother, who had experienced an hysterical
paraplegia and a 'nervous breakdown' as a young woman,
said he was depressed. A psychiatrist called to the house
agreed, recommending phenelzine. After some weeks the
suicide returned to work without explanation. Six months
before his death he left his job as a printing machine operator
without giving a reason. He refused all other employment
offered by the labour exchange, so did not get unemployment
benefit, and not being certified by his doctor as off sick meant
he had no income. He spent the time driving about in an
untaxed, uninsured car without a driving licence. He was due

to appear in court on charges arising from this conduct 3 days after he died, with a strong chance of imprisonment for not paying fines from previous convictions.

The unemployment evidently arises from his mood disorder which, although apparently a permanent personality trait, became worse at times of strain, the recent episode being related to his mother's death 18 months before his own.

The consequences of illness are reflected in sickness absence from work. Here the suicides showed more absence in the year before their death than did the controls for the year before their interview. Fifty-six per cent of suicides had been off work for more than 2 weeks in the year, compared to 19 per cent of controls. The conditions which kept the suicides off work were mental illness and alcoholism.

A case history shows how recurrent depression caused sickness absence:

A married man of 60 killed himself with 2 grams of pentobarbitone. He lived happily with his wife and had been employed 17 years as a coppersmith, a well-regarded skilled man. The first episode of depression occurred at age 30, and further episodes at 50, 52, 56 and 58, the last four requiring inpatient treatment with drugs and ECT. Three weeks before death depressive symptoms recurred and he stopped work with a medical sickness certificate from his doctor.

Frequent changes of job may be the outcome of illness or of an unstable personality. A third of the suicides had held three or more jobs in the previous 3 years. The reasons for losing jobs were not known in most cases, but in those where it was, drink, drugs and irritability had played a prominent part, not redundancy.

The economically inactive

Within the economically inactive group, similar proportions of suicides and controls were retired, or economically inactive in other ways, such as being a housewife or student. Of the retired group, nine of the 14 suicides (64 per cent) had left work before the official retirement age compared with nine of the 24 controls

(35 per cent). Mental illness accounted for the excessive numbers of early retirements among the suicides, four (29 per cent) having left work prematurely for that reason. A case history illustrates how mental illness can have this effect:

A retired local government officer killed himself when aged 73. His successful career suffered a setback with his first episode of depression at age 51. After three further episodes of depression, each requiring inpatient treatment, he retired at 59 on grounds of mental ill-health. The manic depressive psychosis continued, only partly controlled medically, with three further depressive and two manic episodes, and much mood variation between discrete episodes of illness, until the final episode of depression, when he gassed himself.

After early retirement, health and temperament influenced continued employment. Five of the nine retired controls, but none of the nine retired suicides, had small part-time jobs.

Occupations with high suicide rates

Some occupations are known to have high suicide rates. We assessed the occupations of the economically active suicides and controls, dividing them into those with SMRs of <90, 90–110 and >110. Of the 36 suicides with classifiable occupations, 18 (50 per cent) had occupations with high SMRs compared to 14 (19 per cent) of the 72 controls whose occupations could be classified. Similar proportions of suicides and controls had occupations with SMRs between 90 and 110, but fewer suicides (25 per cent) compared to controls (53 per cent) had occupations with low SMRs.

This inquiry, undertaken in a time of full employment, shows suicides to have much poorer work histories than controls as measured by failure in employment, a fairly gross index. More refined measures, absence from work due to sickness and increased job mobility, also distinguished suicides from controls. Mental illness, alcoholism and psychopathic behaviour seemed to be the direct cause.

MIGRATION

Migration here means a move of residence, a definition which includes in its range a move of house within a neighbourhood and leaving one country for another; and in the scope of its effect encompasses both modest alterations and profound, far-reaching changes to lifestyle. The fact of migration is an indirect measure of a number of real, disparate and interacting influences on a person, which might increase the risk of suicide, as the following brief account attempts to show.

The move might be the outcome of mental illness, alcoholism, or psychopathic disorder, which themselves have high suicide rates. Bereavement or marital disruption, events known to be associated with an increased suicide rate, may also result in migration.

The adjustment to a new environment which migration requires might produce psychological symptoms, or exaggerate those of existing mental illness, increasing the likelihood of suicide. Depending on distance travelled, and the familiarity of the new community, moving may result in a partial or complete loss of the social support of relations, neighbourhood and work, changes which from the Durkheimian standpoint are likely to increase the suicide rate of those affected. Whether the move is forced, for political reasons say, or voluntary, to better employment for example, may have an important influence on whether successful adjustment follows.

Some of the possible causes of an association between migration and suicide are themselves associated, giving rise to the likelihood of complicated, indirect links between migration and suicide. Alcoholism, for instance, has a high suicide rate. Alcoholism also has a high divorce rate, a high rate of psychopathic disorder and a high migration rate. Which of these might determine an increased risk of suicide? Or do they interact? The effects of migration are not confined to the migrants themselves. Large numbers of migrants might influence the suicide-proneness of the host population.

The purpose of this discussion is to look at evidence concerning migration and suicide to determine if migrants have an increased risk of suicide, and if so to assess the possible reasons for it. International migration and moves within a country are both considered.

Migrants to the United States of America have higher suicide rates than their countries of origin (Dublin, 1963). All eleven countries listed in Table 5.1, which is based on data from Dublin, show this phenomenon. Migrants to Australia also have higher rates than their countries of origin (Sainsbury, 1983). International migration is clearly associated with an increased suicide rate.

The cause of the increased suicide risk cannot be inferred from these data. An improved method of ascertaining suicide in the host country compared with that of the native country has been ruled out (Sainsbury, 1983). The possibly greater age of the migrant group compared with that of their native country may contribute a small amount of the increase, but the most plausible hypothesis involves the social consequences of living in a new society.

Is migration within a country associated with suicide? The city centre, an area of high population movement, has a high suicide rate, an observation made for many Western cities. Sainsbury (1955) showed that the suicide rate of the boroughs into which London is divided for local government purposes correlated with the proportions of their residents who were native-born, who had moved there from other parts of Britain or were migrants from abroad. The highest rates were those of the city centre boroughs with the greatest immigration. This suggested migrants had high suicide rates, or that a higher level of migration increased the risk of suicide for the host community.

Using the coroners' inquest documents on suicides, Sainsbury showed that the proportion of suicides who were migrants was far greater than the proportion of the population who were migrants. He concluded that being a migrant increased the risk of suicide.

The increased rate of suicide of the city centre boroughs was not entirely due to migrant deaths, suggesting some other factors enhanced risk of suicide for non-migrants. One of these might be the altered social environment caused by a high proportion of migrants in the population.

A relationship between migration and suicide also exists for the smaller cities and towns of England and Wales. The 1961 Census measured the duration of residence of each member of the population and whether, if they had moved residence within a year, it was within their local authority boundary or from outside it. I correlated these migration statistics with the suicide rates of the 83 cities, called county boroughs at the time, for which they were published, to see if high levels of migration were related to suicide.

The suicide rate for women correlated positively ($r=0.4$) with the percentage of women who had recently moved into their local authority area (Table 4.7). In contrast the percentages of people moving out of a borough, within a borough and the percentage of men moving into a borough did not correlate with borough suicide rates. This finding suggests recent migration from a distance increases the suicide risk for women, but not for men, and that loss of people from a population, and migration over a short distance, does not affect the suicide risk of men or women.

Table 4.7: Correlation between Rates of Suicide and Percentage of Population Resident for a Year or Less by Place of Previous Residence for 83 County Boroughs of England and Wales (1961 Census)

Percentage moving	Males r	Females r
Into borough	0.1	0.4*
Within borough	0.1	0.1
Out of borough	0.1	0.1

* $p< 0.001$; d.f. = 82.

When county borough suicide rates are correlated with duration of residence, the correlation coefficients for women have a pattern, being positive for shorter periods of residence and negative for the longer periods (Table 4.8). For men the correlation is positive for one period only, residence for 3–5 years, a finding which may be due to chance considering the number of correlations calculated for the suicide rate and the absence of a systematic relationship as there is for women.

These findings suggest an increased suicide risk for women who have recently migrated from a distance, a risk which decreases over time. Long residence, or being a native, may protect against suicide. The absence of a measurable association for men is puzzling. The fact of men going out of the home to work, providing an alternative society to that of the home and neighbourhood which, the only society available to most

Table 4.8: Correlation between Rates of Suicide and Duration of Residence of Men and Women in 83 County Boroughs of England and Wales (1961 Census)

Duration of residence (years)	Males r	Females r
< 1	0.13	0.35**
1–2	0.09	0.37**
3–5	0.28*	0.32**
6–15	0.14	−0.01
> 15	−0.19	−0.05
Since birth	−0.18	−0.45**

* $p< 0.01$; ** $p< 0.001$; d.f. = 82.

women, is lost on migration, may be part of the explanation for the difference.

To examine the relation between migration and suicide in more detail requires a case study method, based on interviewing relatives. The remainder of the discussion is therefore concerned with the 75 suicides and their 150 controls.

The duration of residence at the last address for the suicides was compared with that at the time of interview for the controls. Five times as many suicides (27 per cent) as controls (5 per cent) had lived less than 12 months at their last address, and twice as many suicides (13 per cent) as controls (7 per cent) had been there between 1 and 2 years. In contrast, fewer suicides had lived long periods at their last addresses compared to controls (Table 4.9). All age and sex groups were represented in the excess of migrants.

An examination of the number of moves of residence in the previous 5 years showed 33 per cent of suicides to have moved twice or more, compared with 11 per cent of controls (Table 4.10). Suicides are therefore more likely to be migrants, and frequent migrants. The period of vulnerability appears to be the 2 years following a move.

The consequences of moving, evaluated by comparison with the control group, suggest a relative failure of social integration. The suicides who moved were more likely to be living alone, often the consequence of bereavement or marital breakdown, not to be living with a spouse and not to have relations living within a 10-minute journey. They also complained more of

Table 4.9: Duration of Residence for Suicides ($N = 75$) and Controls ($N = 150$)

Years of residence	Suicides		Controls	
	N	%	%	N
< 1	20	27	5	7
1– 2	10	13	7	10
3– 5	13	17	25	38
5–10	8	11	21	32
> 10	24	32	42	63
Total	75	100	100	150

Table 4.10: Number of Moves of House in Past 5 Years for Suicides ($N = 75$) and Controls ($N = 150$)

Number of moves	Suicides		Controls	
	N	%	%	N
None	32	43	63	94
One	18	24	27	40
Two	8	11	7	10
More than three	17	23	4	6

loneliness. These impoverished family ties are likely to aggravate the adverse effects of moving house.

Psychiatric disorder appeared to be the cause of the frequent change of address for some suicides. Those who had moved three or more times in the 5 years before they died were characterised by diagnoses of alcoholism and personality disorder, past histories of suicide attempts and conflicts with the law.

The case study approach shows there is an excess of migrants among suicides, and that migration appears to have weakened the social bonds of those suicides who have moved, and in that way probably increased their predisposition to suicide. There is also a group of suicides who move often because of mental disorder, which is the likely cause of both the move and the suicide.

Conclusion

Migration, whether from one country to another or within one country, is associated with an increased risk of suicide. The cause of the association is uncertain. Both mental illness and social isolation are involved, their relative contribution varying depending on diagnosis.

LIFE EVENTS

Life events are discrete changes to a person's social or physical environment or to their health. Events can be defined, and to some extent ranked for severity of impact. Clinical observations that life events have a temporal relation to the onset of illness, especially mental illness, suggest a causal association, at least in part. The association is established for schizophrenia and deliberate self-harm, perhaps for depression, but not for suicide.

History, literature and the daily paper provide ample examples of suicide following a 'life event'. People appear to 'understand' suicide following personal disasters, even though virtually everyone survives such experiences without resort to suicide.

Published accounts of uncontrolled studies suggest, through lists of unpleasant occurrences, that people who kill themselves have an unusual frequency of adverse life events shortly before they die. But since these reports use the coroner's inquest notes for their facts, they must in part reflect the practice, common to many cultures, of 'explaining' suicide as an understandable response to adversity.

Much of the material already set out in this chapter concerns particular life events, and shows that suicides have more of them than they should. The events already considered are those frequent enough, when counted over a shortish period, to test an hypothesis on a small sample.

In this section of the chapter all those life events which can be defined and counted for a year before a suicide will be considered collectively. This includes the infrequent as well as the more common.

Some comments about method are pertinent. The official coroner's inquiry overcomes three formidable problems of method, which have not been entirely solved for life event work with mental illness: suicide is independently defined; its occurrence can usually be timed within a day; all cases occurring within set geographical boundaries are included.

Deciding the independence of the life event from the phenomenon being studied, a serious problem with other life event work, is not necessary. The act of suicide cannot have caused an event which occurred beforehand. Early and undiagnosed depression, in contrast, can change behaviour and so cause life events. The events may therefore appear to precede the onset of the depression and be inferred as a cause of it.

Discovering and dating all conceivable events for a period preceding a suicide, in the absence of the chief witness, is impossible. The inquiry about life events is accordingly confined to documented events, and those significant enough to be remembered and dated by witnesses, usually close relations. The effect on comprehensiveness of using witnesses instead of the subject, the suicide, is unknown. Events known only to the suicide can never be discovered. Other events, especially those of a shameful or disgraceful nature and which are not public, may be concealed by witnesses. Such events are likely to be underestimated. Other events may be overestimated by witnesses trying to explain the suicide to themselves. However, for the 30 events inquired about, listed in Appendix 3, the inter-rater reliability was high for both the suicides and the controls. Further, the interviewing of a control subject produced the same material as interviewing a witness about the control (Bunch et al., 1971a), suggesting that the events inquired for were easy to define and to remember accurately.

Why should life events precede suicide? In theory there seem to be three ways in which events might predispose to, or cause, suicide:

1. Events might cause or precipitate a mental illness which has a high suicide rate.
2. Events might render the mentally ill vulnerable to suicide by psychological impact, or by disrupting protective social relationships.
3. Events of particular kinds might cause suicidal thoughts and actions, related to cultural values of appropriate conduct, in the absence of illness.

If any, or all, of these are true, life events should, collectively, occur more often before suicide as measured by an appropriate standard. To test this prediction we compared the life events occurring in the 12 months before the suicide for the 75 suicides, with those for the 12 months before the interview for the 150 controls.

The total of events, each counted separately, shows suicides to have 212 events, a mean of 2.8 each, compared to 79 for the controls, a mean of 0.5 each (Table 4.11). Numbers of events experienced per person ranged between zero and twelve for the suicides, zero and four for controls. Fourteen suicides (19 per cent) had five and more events. Only 14 suicides (19 per cent) had no events compared to 98 controls (65 per cent). Suicides therefore had many more events than controls, and there were more suicides with multiple events and fewer with no events than controls.

Those suicides scored as without events may not have been free of their influence. For some, an obvious key event occurred outside the period of inquiry of 12 months, such as the parental bereavement discussed earlier which appeared to exert an influence for at least 4 years. Others experienced an important event which was not one of the 30 defined categories which could be scored for all, such as the birth of an illegitimate child to a mistress.

The frequency distributions have different shapes. The control curve approximates a Poisson distribution, conforming to the theoretical expectation for random infrequent events. But the suicide curve is of a shape suggesting that events are not independent, either being associated because of a common cause, or because one event led to another. Case material suggests both explanations may be true. An example shows how an apparently improbably high number of events can occur:

The suicide, aged 39 when he died from a barbiturate overdose, lived with his divorced wife and three children. The following events occurred in the year before he died:

Lost employment
Wife obtained legal separation
Wife divorced him
Son born
Children taken into care
Children returned home on a supervision order

Table 4.11: Frequency Distribution of Numbers of Life Events in Previous Year, for Suicides (N = 75) and Controls (N = 150)

	Numbers of events														
	0	1	2	3	4	5	6	7	8	9	10	11	12	Total	Mean
Suicide															
N	14	16	10	11	10	2	6	2	0	0	2	1	1	212	2.83
%	19	21	13	15	13	3	8	3	0	0	3	1	1		
Control															
%	65	21	10	2	1	0	0	0	0	0	0	0	0	79	0.53
N	98	32	15	3	2	0	0	0	0	0	0	0	0		

Child referred to child guidance clinic
Duodenal ulcer recurrence diagnosed
Slashed wrists deliberately
Convicted and awaiting sentence for theft
Wife discovered getting goods on false pretences

These events occurred in a setting of serious medical and psychiatric illness and related social problems.

Renal disease of 18 years' duration resulted in a nephrectomy 5 years before death. The remaining kidney was sound. Duodenal ulcer diagnosed 8 years earlier resulted in a vagotomy and gastro-enterostomy 4 years before death. An ulcer recurrence was diagnosed shortly before death, but not confirmed at postmortem.

Psychiatric disturbance had four aspects. Psychopathic personality disorder diagnosed because of repeated crime (14 convictions for petty theft), violence and lying. Alcohol, barbiturate and analgesic abuse present for many years. Episodes of depression severe enough for psychiatric treatment. Deliberate self-harm, four instances.

The breakdown of the marriage and his mother's death, 4 years before the suicide, left an overdependent man without psychological support. His conduct alienated relatives and friends. Money was short, and prison likely.

The common factor determining nine of the events listed, the behaviour of the suicide, also contributed to the medical and psychiatric illnesses and to the social difficulties.

To examine the time relation between events and suicide, events were timed to the quarter of the year preceding the suicide or the control interview (Table 4.12).

In each quarter suicides have more events than controls. The events for controls occur at the same rate each quarter; in contrast the rate of occurrence of events for suicide shows an increase in rate through the 12 months and then an acceleration near the date of the death.

Events forecast to take place after the suicide or after the control interview, for example the wedding to occur the day following the suicide of the bride's mother, and the court appearance on a theft charge a week after the suicide, were also more frequent for the suicides than the controls.

Table 4.12: Chronology of Life Events for Suicides (*N* = 75) and Controls (*N* = 150)

Number of events	Quarters of the year				I	Future
	Past					
	4th	3rd	2nd	1st		1st
90–						
80–				S		
70–				S		
60–				S		
50–			S	S		
40–			S	S		
30–		S	S	S		
20–	S	S	S	S		
10–	C S	C S	C S	C S		
0–	C S	C S	C S	C S		S

S = Suicide; C = control; I = day of suicide or control interview.

Events can be classified according to the department of life they most influence and in which they arise. The classification, although to some extent arbitrary because some events affect many aspects of life, can show if some spheres of life are affected more than others (Table 4.13).

Table 4.13: Rate per Person of Life Events, in Previous Year, by 'Life Area', for Suicides (*N* = 75) and Controls (*N* = 150)

	S (*N* = 75)	C (*N* = 150)
Work	0.85	0.17
Household	0.76	0.11
Psychiatric	0.35	0.00
Medical	0.27	0.11
Neighbourhood	0.27	0.05
Legal	0.13	0.00
Death	0.16	0.09
Other	0.07	0.01

Work and household, the most commonly occurring type of event for both suicide and controls, was five to six times more frequent for the suicides. Events concerning mental ill-health were next most common for the suicides, none occurring for the controls. The finding is to some extent an artefact because the control group definition excluded those having treatment from a psychiatrist at the time of the interview. This resulted in the replacement of two controls having outpatient psychiatric care. Even with their inclusion the suicide group has vastly more events related to mental illness. Neighbourhood events, mainly related to moving house, occurred five times more often in the suicides than in the controls. Medical events, concerned with physical as opposed to mental illness, and bereavements, were more evenly divided between suicides and controls, although still commoner among the suicides.

Conclusion

Life events, as predicted, occurred more commonly among the suicides than the controls, being some five times more frequent in the year before the death. Events increased in frequency throughout the year, the rate of occurrence accelerating before the suicide. The events were those mainly affecting, or arising from within, the suicide's household or from mental ill-health.

The relation between life events and suicide is more complicated than the relation between life events and mental illness. That is because most suicides are mentally ill at their death, and the event may have played a part in causing the illness, the suicide, or both. Further, illness behaviour, or conduct arising from an abnormal personality, may result in events which change the social environment unfavourably, worsening the outlook for the illness, inducing depressed mood, and enhancing the risk of suicide.

5

Accuracy of the Suicide Rate

Durkheim, in *Le Suicide* (Durkheim, 1897), asserted that the suicide rate of any society is not merely the sum of individual acts of suicide occurring in isolation, but reflects the character of that society as a whole. Investigation of the causes of suicide therefore requires study of a community's social structures, and may enable inferences to be drawn about the effects of cultural factors, for example religious practice and belief, upon the suicide rate.

Such investigations, which involve comparing the suicide rates of different societies, are pointless unless it can be shown that differences between the official rates for these societies are valid, and not the result of variation in ascertainment procedure: that is, the process intervening between finding a body and writing 'suicide' on a death certificate. The error from compiling national statistics from death certificates is not taken into account in this argument, being considered clerical in origin and therefore unbiased.

The problem is not unique to the study of suicide. All epidemiological research needs to be based on valid and reliable definitions of disease which are independent of variations in local practice. Ascertainment of suicide, however, does pose unique problems. The evidence supporting suicide as the cause of death is sometimes not strong enough to provide proof, and in some cultures the stigma and religious condemnation attached to this form of death may lead probable suicides for which the slightest doubt exists to be classified to other causes of death. The suicide statistics of Arab countries may illustrate this type of bias. Kuwait, for instance, has a suicide rate of 0.1 per 100,000, one of the lowest in the world.

The accuracy of suicide rates has frequently been questioned, even in Durkheim's time. Durkheim, in an interesting contrast to the sociologist of today, appears to have accepted the accuracy of suicide statistics to the point of naivety. Over the past 20 years, coinciding with a great increase of interest in suicide, this questioning has intensified, the most forceful critics being sociologists and psychologists. Some of the writings of today's behavioural scientists, which criticise suicide statistics almost to the point of destruction, seem to ignore the importance of Durkheim's contribution on suicide to their subject. One line of criticism is that coroners, and their equivalents, will return suicide verdicts only in the presence of the stereotyped features associated with suicide: mental illness, distressing circumstances, and social isolation. These features are then 'discovered' by research workers, who publish results which are read by coroners, and so the circular process continues. A criticism of greater significance is that a community's attitude — whether suicide is stigmatised, abhorred, tolerated, or even admired — will bring about covert behaviour leading to greater or lesser degrees of concealment after a suicide has occurred. A low suicide rate might therefore be measuring nothing more than a society's disapproval of suicide and ability to conceal suicides by having them certified as some other form of death. These critics therefore argue that suicide rates are useless artefacts of the ascertainment procedure, reflecting preconceived stereotypes and prejudices, without any important relation to the real incidence of suicide.

There can be little doubt that these criticisms have some merit but the issue is whether, in the modern state, their influence is significant enough to outweigh valid differences of suicide incidence, should these exist. No scientific measurement is completely accurate, and the suicide rate is no exception, though for suicide the direction of the error is known, which is not the case for most causes of death. The official rate in England and Wales underestimates the incidence of suicide because of the strict legal definition which English coroners are obliged to use, and perhaps because of their desire to avoid stigmatising the surviving family. The same influence is reported for many other countries.

This chapter describes inquiries designed to find out if suicide rate differences between countries, and between English county boroughs, reflect variations in the real incidence of suicide rather than variations in ascertainment processes.

INTERNATIONAL COMPARISONS

The first study (Sainsbury and Barraclough, 1968) was based on the suicide rates for immigrants to the United States of America from eleven other countries. The immigrants had died in the United States and their deaths were dealt with by the American ascertainment procedures, not those of their country of birth. The rates differed considerably — the highest being 34.2 per 100,000 for immigrants born in Sweden, and the lowest 7.9 per 100,000 for those born in Mexico. The rank order of these eleven suicide rates was compared with the rank order of the suicide rates published by the eleven countries of origin. The correlation between the two was high ($r = 0.87$, $p<0.001$) (Table 5.1), though the rank orders were not identical. People born in Sweden, Austria, Czechoslovakia, or the German Federal Republic were recorded as having a high suicide rate whether they died in their own country or in the United States; and low rates were recorded for those born in Ireland or Mexico, whether they died in the parent country or the adopted one.

Table 5.1: Suicide Rates per 100,000 of US Foreign-born and of their Countries of Origin (1959)

	Suicide rate of foreign born	Rank	Rank	Suicide rate of country of origin
Sweden	34	1	4	18
Austria	33	2	1	25
Czechoslovakia	32	3	1	25
Federal Republic of Germany	26	4	3	19
Poland	25	5	5	8
Norway	24	6	5	8
England	19	7	7	11
Italy	18	8	8	6
Canada	17	9	9	7
Ireland	10	10	10	3
Mexico	8	11	11	2

$r = 0.87$; $p < 0.001$; US suicide rate = 10 per 100,000

The finding that the international differences persisted shows that the differences between the rates of the original countries cannot be accounted for by differences in their individual national procedures. Each immigrant group had carried its

95

suicide rate with it to the new country. This phenomenon had already been noted in the 1920s for immigrants living in New York State, and is mentioned by Dublin (1963). Study of the suicide rate for immigrants to Australia reveals equivalent findings (Sainsbury, 1983). A similar phenomenon has also been observed for certain diseases, multiple sclerosis for instance.

All the immigrant groups examined had higher suicide rates than those of their parent countries. The higher suicide rates for the immigrant groups cannot be accounted for by the United States procedure being more liberal in its definition of suicide, since the immigrant groups included those with both higher and lower rates than the United States as a whole. The raised rate is probably the result of some pervasive influence affecting immigrant groups, such as the difficulties of adjusting to a new way of life, the older age of the immigrant group or the personality traits which lead people to migrate voluntarily. Links between migration and suicide are discussed in Chapter 4.

It is interesting to speculate on the cause of an immigrant group carrying its suicide rate with it. There appear to be three possible mechanisms. The social structure of a group, if maintained in the new environment, could mediate the tendency to suicide. The young of a society might learn ways of thinking and behaving before migration which determine their vulnerability to suicide, and then carry these with them to the new country. Or those who decide to uproot themselves may do so because of personality traits or early symptoms of mental illness peculiar to their culture, and which predispose to suicide. The possibility that immigrant groups also carry with them the capacity to conceal suicide from the authorities in their new country, thus accounting for low rates, has not been refuted but seems far-fetched.

Doubtful suicides, and deaths which are almost certainly suicides on common-sense grounds but for which there is not enough evidence of intent to fulfil the legal definition of suicide, are classified as undetermined deaths, which are therefore a large part of the error of the suicide rate. The sum of the suicide rate and the undetermined rate may provide a better estimate of the 'true' suicide rate than does the official suicide rate alone. A further test of the hypothesis that the rank order of the suicide rates of nations is independent of ascertainment procedures can therefore be made by comparing their rank order for the suicide rate with their rank order for the suicide rate plus the undetermined death rate. This procedure was carried out for a sample of 22 countries which published mortality statistics in the *World Health Statistics Annual* (Barraclough, 1973) (Table 5.2). Again, a high correlation was found (rho=0.89, $p<0.001$). Whichever method was used, West Berlin had the highest rate and Malta the lowest. That the 40-fold difference between the suicide rates of these modern states results from differences in ascertainment procedures is hardly credible.

These two studies, in demonstrating that the rank order of the suicide rates of different countries is virtually independent of their individual ascertainment procedures, provide strong evidence that differences between official suicide rates for modern states reflect real differences in incidence of suicide. Ascertainment procedures may, however, affect the magnitude of differences between national rates even if their influence is not great enough to affect the rank order, and the following section describes studies of this phenomenon within the three states which comprise the British Isles, excepting Northern Ireland.

COMPARISONS WITHIN THE BRITISH ISLES

Long-standing differences exist between the official suicide rates for England and Wales, Scotland, and Eire. The mortality statistics of these countries are among the most comprehensive in the world, they share a common language and their geographical proximity enables their systems for classifying violent deaths to be investigated at first hand. These common features provide an excellent opportunity for detailed study of how ascertainment procedures affect official suicide statistics.

The first inquiry compared England and Wales with Scotland (Barraclough, 1972a). The Scottish suicide rate had been lower than the English for over 70 years — surprising because the social characteristics of the two countries are not so dissimilar. The discrepancy in their official suicide rates, which is of the order of 20 per cent and has been the subject of much speculation, could be an artefact of the very different ascertain-

Table 5.2: Suicide Rates and Undetermined Death Rates per 100,000 for 22 Countries (1968)

Country	Suicide rate (AE 147)	Rank	Rank	Undetermined rate plus suicide rate	Undetermined rate (AE 149)
West Berlin	42.7	1	1	42.8	0.1
Belgium	15.5	2	4	15.5	—
France	15.3	3	3	20.6	5.3
Japan	14.4	4	5	15.2	0.8
Australia	12.7	5	6	14.5	1.8
Yugoslavia	12.6	6	7	13.1	0.5
USA	10.7	7	8	12.8	2.1
Bulgaria	9.9	8	12	10.2	0.3
New Zealand	9.6	9	13	9.9	0.3
England and Wales	9.4	10	10.5	11.9	2.5
Salvador	8.2	11	9	12.1	3.9
Chile	8.1	12	2	32.3	24.2
Scotland	7.2	13	10.5	11.9	4.7
Northern Ireland	6.6	14	17	7.4	0.8
Venezuela	6.1	15	15	8.2	2.1
Panama	3.9	16	16	7.9	4.0
Greece	3.6	17	20	5.0	1.4
Barbados	3.2	18	18	5.6	2.4
Dominica	3.1	19	14	9.5	6.4
Ireland	2.4	20	19	5.4	3.0
Mexico	1.6	21	21	1.6	—
Malta	0.9	22	22	1.5	0.6

rho = 0.89, $p < 0.001$.
Suicide rate rank correlated with undetermined rate plus suicide rate, rank.

ment procedures in the two countries. These procedures will therefore be described.

In England and Wales, statistics about unnatural deaths are compiled from death certificates which have been completed by coroners following a public inquiry, the inquest. Coroners are judicial officers of the Crown whose main functions are to investigate unnatural deaths in their districts and to improve standards of death certification. They are largely independent of local and central authority. Ninety per cent of coroners are lawyers, 5 per cent doctors, and 5 per cent are qualified in both medicine and law. Nearly all are men. Except in large districts their coroner's duties are part-time and usually combined with a solicitor's practice. Before an inquest is held into a death which appears to be unnatural, the coroner's officer assembles the facts about the case. Coroners' officers are experienced policemen seconded to this duty, usually for several years. The coroner's officer collects written statements from witnesses, and arranges, after consultation with the coroner, for a postmortem to be carried out. Postmortems are held for some 80 per cent of suicide cases. At the inquest, a formal procedure which must be public and is usually held in a courtroom, the coroner examines witnesses under oath to amplify their written statements, and hears expert evidence. After consideration of all the facts he considers relevant, the coroner records all unnatural deaths, with the exception of homicides, to one of three categories: suicide, accident, or open verdict. Open verdict deaths, in which the coroner considers the evidence insufficient to enable him to decide between suicide and accident, appear as 'undetermined deaths' in mortality statistics. The essential part of the legal definition of suicide, rooted in the Common Law and reiterated from time to time in High Court hearings of contested coroners' decisions, is 'there should be some actual evidence pointing to the event: the verdict should not rest upon surmise' (Purchase and Wollaston, 1957; Burton, Chambers and Gill, 1985). The possibility of a quashed verdict influences coroners not to record a death as suicide unless the evidence is substantial. Unlike doctors certifying deaths from natural causes, coroners cannot use a common-sense definition based on the balance of probabilities. Some coroners are reluctant to use an open verdict even when there is no clear evidence to enable them to decide between suicide and accident, since they feel it is unjust to the deceased's memory, or to the relatives, not to have a clear decision. Coroners who take this view may be inclined to class the doubtful suicide to accidental death. A fuller consideration of these matters is given in Chapter 6.

In Scotland, at the time this inquiry was made, suicide statistics were compiled from death certificates completed after procedures of Byzantine complexity, which have hardly changed since. Unnatural deaths are investigated by locally based Procurators Fiscal, legally trained civil servants mainly concerned with criminal matters and responsible to the Crown Office in Edinburgh which administers the Criminal Law in Scotland. A postmortem is carried out in 50 per cent of cases, compared with 80 per cent in England. A précis of the Fiscal's report is examined at the Crown Office by Crown Counsel to decide whether there is a need for criminal proceedings. Some deaths are classified as suicide at this stage and notified to the Registrar General's office anonymously, to preserve confidentiality. Other unnatural deaths are classified as suicide by the Registrar General's office using information from its own inquiries. The rest are classified as accidents or undetermined. No official definition of suicide is published, nor can suicide decisions be contested in the courts, as they can in England. The definition in use at the Crown Office is stated to be 'there must be clear evidence that the deceased took his own life', similar to the English one though perhaps stricter. The definition used in the Scottish Registrar General's office is not known.

The English and Scottish procedures therefore differ in the quantity of written and verbal information available to the person who decides the cause of death, whether the inquiry is public or private, and the possibility of the verdict being judicially reversed. An indirect influence could be that the Scottish jury verdict of 'not proven' in criminal cases, which has no English equivalent, may make an undetermined or open verdict more acceptable to the Scottish lawyers of the Crown Office than it is to English coroners.

These differences in ascertainment procedure are likely to result in a higher proportion of self-inflicted deaths being classed as undetermined in Scotland than in England and Wales. This is the case. In 1963 the undetermined death rate was 63 per million in Scotland compared with 30 in England. The suicide rate was 97 per million in Scotland compared with 123 in England and Wales (Barraclough, 1972a).

Since the bias favours the doubtful suicide being classified to undetermined death, and the doubtful accident to accidental death, deaths recorded as undetermined are likely to be suicides of varying degrees of uncertainty. If this is so, the real difference in the incidence of suicide between Scotland and England and Wales must be less than the 26 per million indicated by the official suicide rates. The difference between the sum of the suicide and undetermined death rates for the two countries is probably a better estimate of any true difference in the frequency of suicide. Adding the two rates for the population aged 15 and over for 1968 produces a total of 160 per million in Scotland and 153 per million in England and Wales, suggesting that the difference in the official suicide rates of the two countries is largely an artefact of their different ascertainment procedures (Table 5.3)

A similar approach was used to compare the suicide rate of England and Wales with that of Eire (Barraclough, 1978a). According to official statistics, the rate for Eire is four times less than the English one. The accuracy of this rate has often been questioned on the grounds that the unusual stigma attaching to suicide in this Catholic country, even if associated with a genuinely low suicide rate, also leads to concealment or under-reporting of suicide. Eire has a coroner system similar to the English one, and a similar legal definition of suicide is in use there. Differences from the English coroner system are small. Half the coroners are medically qualified, postmortems are carried out on all cases of unnatural death, and the legal definition of suicide seems stricter. The possibility of appealing against a suicide verdict is uncertain.

For 1968–70 the suicide rate for the population aged 15 and over was 29 per million in Eire compared with 123 in England and Wales. The undetermined rate was 44 per million in Eire compared with 30 in England and Wales. The sum of the two rates was therefore 73 per million in Eire compared with 153 in England and Wales. Supposing this sum gives a better estimate of the true suicide rate than the official suicide rate alone, Eire still has an exceptionally low rate, one of the lowest in Europe, but it is about half the English one instead of a quarter of it.

A more sensitive test of the effects of different ascertainment procedures can be devised by examining poisoning mortality statistics. Poisoning suicides, with the exception of those from caustics and corrosives, are often difficult or impossible to distinguish from accidents because fatal poisonings nearly

Table 5.3: Suicide Rates, Undetermined Death Rates and Accidental Death Rates (Selected Causes) Per Million for England and Wales and for Scotland, 1968, for the Population aged 15 and over

	Numbers		Rates		Difference in rates	Twice s.e. of difference in the rates
	England and Wales	Scotland	England and Wales	Scotland		
All causes of death						
*Suicide rate (S.R.)	4,580	373	123	97	26	11
*Undetermined rate (U.R.)	1,130	241	30	63	33	8
*Accident rate (A.R.)	1,364	173	37	45	8	7
*S.R. + U.R. + A.R.	7,074	787	190	205	15	15
*A.R. + U.R.	2,494	414	67	108	41	11
S.R. + U.R.	5,710	614	153	160	7	14
Death caused by firearms, cutting, piercing, jumping, falling and hanging						
S.R.	984	90	26	23	3	5
*U.R.	92	18	2	5	3	2
*A.R.	163	35	4	9	5	3
S.R. + U.R. + A.R.	1,239	143	32	37	5	7
*A.R. + U.R.	255	53	6	14	8	4
S.R. + U.R.	1,076	108	28	28	0	6
Death caused by poisoning, gassing, drowning						
*S.R.	3,416	273	92	71	21	9
*U.R.	881	219	24	57	33	8
*A.R.	1,071	92	29	24	5	5
S.R. + U.R. + A.R.	5,368	584	144	152	8	13
*A.R. + U.R.	1,952	311	52	81	29	10
*S.R. + U.R.	4,297	492	115	128	13	12

* Indicates a difference in the rates significant at 5 per cent.

always take place in private. Definite evidence of intent cannot be inferred from the method itself in the way which is possible for more violent methods such as hanging, because the size of the dose is hard to determine accurately. Even when a large dose has undoubtedly been taken, there remains the possibility of accidental overdose while drowsy. Mortality statistics for poisoning by drugs and chemicals are published annually, giving the numbers of deaths for each drug. For 1968–70 the percentage distribution of poisoning deaths in 27 classes of drug was virtually the same in Scotland as it was in England and Wales (Barraclough, 1974b). The 3-year average death rate from poisoning, irrespective of the verdict, for those over 15 years of age was 77 per million in each country. But the proportions of poisonings classified as suicide or undetermined deaths in the two countries differed; the suicide rate from poisoning, 42 per million in Scotland compared with 50 in England and Wales, contrasted with the undetermined death rate from poisoning, 29 per million in Scotland compared with 14 in England and Wales (Table 5.4).

Table 5.4: Poisoning Deaths, 3-year Average Rates per Million of Population aged over 15, Classified as Suicide (E950), Undetermined (E980), Accident (E850–869) and Total (N960–979, 980–985, 988, 989), Scotland, and England and Wales, 1968, 1969, 1970

	Scotland		England and Wales		Difference in rates	Twice s.e. of difference
	Rate	N	Rate	N		
Suicide*	42	(482)	50	(5,637)	8	4
Undetermined*	29	(333)	14	(1,547)	15	3
Accident*	7	(76)	13	(1,451)	6	1
Total	77	(891)	77	(8,635)	0	6

* Difference in rates significant at 1 per cent level.

Twice as many deaths from barbiturate poisoning are classified as undetermined in Scotland as England (Table 5.5), a finding in keeping with the conclusion that the Scottish system is inherently biased towards the undetermined verdict. These observations are hard to explain except by differing ascertainment procedures, and suggest that the true incidence of suicide from poisoning is the same in Scotland as it is in England and Wales.

Table 5.5: Classification of Poisoning Deaths by Selected Drug Groups for Scotland, England and Wales, 1968, 1969, 1970, All Ages

	Scotland (%)	England and Wales (%)
N965 (Analgesics and antipyretics)	(N = 59)	(N = 878)
Suicide	48	70
Undetermined	42	15
Accident	10	15
N967.0 (Barbiturates)	(N = 627)	(N = 6,000)
Suicide	57	66
Undetermined	37	19
Accident	7	16
N970 (Psychotherapeutics)	(N = 62)	(N = 713)
Suicide	55	58
Undetermined	31	21
Accident	15	21

INFLUENCES ON THE ENGLISH SUICIDE RATE

The suicide rate for England and Wales is published in the mortality statistics issued by the Office of Population Censuses and Surveys (OPCS). Errors in this official suicide rate could arise at any point in the chain of events, starting with the discovery of a body, which lead to recording of the death as suicide and the collection, collation and publication of statistical material. The suicide rate has fluctuated since the publication of mortality statistics began in 1839. During the twentieth century the lowest rate, 73 per million, recorded in 1917, reflected the reduction in the suicide rate observed in wartime and the highest rate, 137 per million in 1934, nearly double the lowest rate, illustrated the rise associated with periods of economic depression. Critics claim the fluctuations in rate are largely artefactual, due to changes in the method of investigating and classifying unnatural deaths during this period. The following section describes inquiries into the extent to which such factors may have influenced the rate.

The most important potential source of variation is the coroner, for he decides if a death is to be classified as suicide.

Suicide was a felony, a serious criminal offence although unpunishable, until 1961. The definition of suicide which the coroner must use reflects this fact, and remains firmly rooted in the legal tradition of the Common Law. Some consequences of the conflict between this tradition and the modern view that death from suicide is not criminal, but medical, will be discussed in Chapter 7 which deals with the aftermath of suicide. The legal definition customarily referred to is that given by Rolfe in 1846 in Clift v. Schwabb: 'Every act of self destruction is, in common language, described by the word suicide provided it be the intentional act of a party knowing the probable consequences of what he is about' (Common Bench Reports 1846: quoted in Thurston, 1976). This judgement is merely a convenient reference in time for the reiteration of long-established Common Law. The up-to-date restatement is provided in *Coroner's Inquiries* (Burton, Chambers and Gill, 1985) R. v. Cardiff City Coroner ex parte Thomas (1970): 'Suicide is voluntarily doing an act for the purpose of destroying one's own life while one is conscious of what one is doing, and in order to arrive at a verdict of suicide there must be evidence that the deceased intended the consequences of his act.'

The law tends to assume that self-destructive behaviour can be classed into definitely suicidal and definitely not suicidal. In practice there is a continuum from the indisputable suicide to the incontestable accident, with a moderate measure of the undecidable occupying the middle ground. Consider these three real cases:

A 64-year-old widowed labourer who lived by himself was found dead in his woodshed holding a shotgun which had blown a hole in his chest. In the house there was a note, dated the same day, addressed to a relative who visited daily, which read 'Don't come down the shed Mary, I shot myself.'

A 50-year-old medical practitioner was found dead in her bedroom fully dressed, 30 minutes after morning surgery was due to begin. The evidence proved she had taken ten tablets each containing 200 mg of amylobarbitone, a potentially fatal dose on an empty stomach, about 45 minutes before her body was found. There was no evidence of recent suicidal thinking or preparations for death, but in the past she had taken many overdoses preceded by episodes of depression.

A 45-year-old woman's body was found in pieces on a railway track. A few hours before she had been admitted to a nearby psychiatric unit with an acute recurrence of a long-standing serious mental illness characterised by depression and agitation. She had been seriously distressed on the ward, evaded the staff and ran away.

Suicide verdicts were returned in the first two cases — for the first an indisputable decision, but for the second an open verdict or even accidental death verdict could have been used. For the third case an open verdict was returned when a suicide verdict might have been more appropriate.

Variation between individual coroners

Is the definition of suicide independent of the coroner? Consistency between different coroners in their use of the term is encouraged in many ways. The legal definition of suicide is published in the coroners' handbook, an authoritative summary of law and practice to which the coroner may refer. The definition is tested from time to time in the High Courts after a suicide or accidental death verdict has been challenged, the outcome of influential cases being published in the Law Reports of the daily newspapers, especially *The Times, Guardian* and *Daily Telegraph*, the professional Law Reports, and the *Journal of the Coroners' Society*. Coroners often serve an apprenticeship as deputy coroners before the full appointment, and so learn the ropes. They meet at local and national meetings of the Coroners' Society, where through informal discussion they maintain an oral tradition of what is and is not a suicide, derived, as might be expected in a profession which values precedent, from the opinion of the older and more experienced man.

The definition of suicide appears so entrenched in the literature and lore of coronership that there should be reasonable uniformity of use in the geographically small and well-administered state of England and Wales. However, variation in individual personality, attitudes and experiences might well lead different coroners to bring different verdicts on borderline cases such as those summarised above.

If the definition of suicide is applied uniformly by coroners, a change of coroner should not influence the suicide rate within a district. Until 1974 urban England and Wales had 79 county boroughs, each with its own coroner and mortality statistics. The rank order of suicide rates for all 79 boroughs for 1950–52 was compared with that for 1960–62 (Barraclough, 1970), and the correlation coefficient was found to be 0.43 ($p<0.001$), indicating that the rank had retained some consistency after a lapse of 10 years. The frequency distribution of their suicide rates was statistically normal. A similar comparison carried out for the 39 boroughs which had kept the same coroner throughout the 10-year period yielded a correlation coefficient of 0.45 ($p<0.01$): and for the 19 boroughs which had had a change of coroner during the intervening 10 years, a correlation coefficient of 0.49 ($p<0.05$). Twenty-one boroughs were omitted because the coroner had changed during one of the 6 years from which rates were obtained (Table 5.6).

Table 5.6: Product–Moment Correlations between the 3-year Average Suicide Rates of County Boroughs*, 1950–2 and 1960–2

	r	p
79 county boroughs	0.43	< 0.001
39 county boroughs	0.45	< 0.01
19 county boroughs	0.49	< 0.05

* Twenty-one boroughs were omitted because the coroner had changed during one of the 6 years from which the rates were obtained.

This result suggests that changes of coroner do not have a significant overall influence on the suicide rate, and that coroners' definition of suicide is a robust one for the purposes of national statistics. When individual boroughs were examined separately, however, there were one or two examples of a large change in rates after a new coroner had taken office. The earlier coroner in one such borough had had a suicide verdict quashed on appeal and the second inquest reversed his decision. The new coroner said he had been much influenced by his predecessor's mortifying experience and as a result he frequently returned open verdicts on deaths which he privately thought were suicides. Consequently his ratio of open verdicts to suicides was very much greater than that of other coroners in the sample.

In the period covered by this study, poisoning by drugs had not yet become the commonest method of suicide. Carbon monoxide poisoning by domestic coal gas accounted for at least half the suicide deaths. Gassing is a method for which suicidal intent is easily inferred, because the suicide has to take deliberate measures to ensure the gas concentration is high enough to be fatal. If the study were repeated now that carbon monoxide poisoning is rare, and over half all cases of suicide result from poisoning with prescribed medicines, less consistency between different coroners might be found.

The effect of individual differences between coroners was studied in more detail for the City of Cambridge Coronership between 1959 and 1974 (Barraclough 1978b). This district had a deputy coroner who took over the work when the coroner was on holiday, and helped at busy periods. Overall, the coroner himself took 77 per cent of cases and his deputy took 23 per cent. If they shared common definitions, the proportions of suicide, open and accidental death verdicts in the cases they heard would be the same. This was not found to be so. Although they brought in similar proportions of suicides the

Table 5.7: Verdicts Given by Coroner and Deputy Coroner, by Cause of Death

	Suicide		Open verdict		Accident		Total	
	N	%	N	%	N	%	N	%
All deaths[a]								
Coroner	132	54	53	22	61	24	246	100
Deputy	44	59	6	8	25	32	75	100
All	176	55	59	18	86	27	321	100
Deaths from poisoning by solid and liquid substances[b]								
Coroner	34	35	39	39	25	26	98	100
Deputy	16	59	2	7	9	33	27	100
All	50	40	41	33	34	27	125	100
Deaths from carbon monoxide, drowning and violent means[c]								
Coroner	98	66	14	9	36	24	148	100
Deputy	28	58	4	8	16	33	48	100
All	126	64	18	9	52	27	196	100

[a] $\chi^2 = 7.56$; d.f. = 2; $p < 0.05$.
[b] $\chi^2 = 10.44$; d.f. = 2; $p < 0.01$.
[c] $\chi^2 = 1.51$; d.f. = 2; $p > 0.2$.

coroner brought in three times more open verdicts than his deputy, this difference being entirely accounted for by the poisoning cases (Table 5.7).

The decision in doubtful cases can be influenced by the coroner's personal outlook, as was made clear in the course of conversation with the two men concerned. The deputy coroner expressed a strong dislike of the open verdict, which he regarded as carrying a stigma for the deceased's relatives. He felt obliged to choose between the verdicts of suicide and accidental death if at all possible. The coroner, in contrast, pointed out that the High Court has made it clear that an open verdict is the appropriate one where doubt exists, and considered that positive proof is required before either a suicide or an accident verdict can be brought in.

The influence of High Court verdicts

Coroners' use of the definition of suicide may be influenced by the results of High Court hearings of appeals against coroners' verdicts, as illustrated in the previous section by the story of the new coroner who had been over-influenced by his predecessor's experience of a quashed verdict. Between 1944 and 1975 there were ten appeals to have verdicts of suicide or accident quashed noticed in Law Reports. Such appeals are a contemporary phenomenon, since the last appeal noticed in the Law Reports before 1944 took place in 1912. The increased frequency of such challenges to the coroner coincides with an increase of interest in suicide from many quarters. Following each appeal, whatever the outcome, the definition of suicide referred to on p. 105 has been reiterated in the High Court, and reported in Law Reports of the professional journals and the quality newspapers. These reports should have the effect of making coroners apply the definition of suicide more stringently, discouraging drift towards a liberal application of the definition based on a common-sense balance of probabilities. Such a tightening of the coroners' operational definition should result in a fall in the suicide rate and a rise in the accident or undetermined rate after the reporting of a High Court appeal.

We examined the time trends in national mortality statistics to see whether this was so (Jennings and Barraclough, 1980). High Court cases in 1944, 1956, 1970 and 1976 were followed by

ACCURACY OF THE SUICIDE RATE

rises in the suicide rate, not falls, which is against the predicted trend. Cases in 1967 and 1968 were followed by falls, but of a size which cannot explain more than a small part of the fall in the suicide rate already under way after the detoxification of household gas. Two cases in 1974 were followed by falls. The absence of any consistent pattern shows that the results of High Court appeals do not exert a substantial influence on the national suicide statistics, and suggest that coroners were already using the definition as tradition prescribed. In the same paper (Jennings and Barraclough, 1980), other legal and administrative innovations which have affected coroners' work since 1900 are examined. These include the reliability of the procedure for investigating suspected suicides, coding by the OPCS, and changes in the law regulating coroners' work, including the relaxation of the requirement for juries in all cases. The findings lead to the conclusion that such changes cannot explain fluctuations in the English suicide rate, fluctuations which must therefore be explained in other ways.

The influence of coroners' officers and pathologists

The evidence for the inquest is collected by coroners' officers, experienced policemen seconded to the coroner usually for some years. Their outlook on suicide could bias the selection of evidence, for example the number and content of statements collected from witnesses and whether a postmortem is done, and so influence the coroner's verdict. The coroner's pathologist who carries out the postmortem could also influence the verdict, according to how thoroughly the examination is made and the interpretation placed on the findings, especially as regards evidence of intent. Both these sources of error were considered in a study of 330 unnatural deaths, in which 110 consecutive open verdict deaths were compared with 110 accidental deaths and 110 suicides matched for age, sex and exact cause of death (Barraclough, Holding and Fayers, 1976). The study will be described in Chapter 6 on the undetermined death. The cases were from the Inner West London coronership, a huge district with a full-time coroner assisted by a staff of 14 full-time coroners' officers and five consultant pathologists. All cases had pathologists' reports.

The distribution of cases to each of the three verdicts did not differ according to which policeman or pathologist was concerned, any more than would be expected by chance (Table 5.8). The poisoning cases, examined separately to provide a more sensitive test, showed no significant differences either. We concluded that the coroners' officers and coroners' pathologists had similar approaches to the collection and presentation of evidence to the coroner, and that individual variations between them are unlikely to influence the official suicide rate. They probably stick to the facts and leave the interpretation to the coroner.

Classifying poisoning deaths

Differentiating suicidal from accidental poisoning is difficult and sometimes impossible. The act of fatal self-poisoning is hardly ever witnessed, and the nature of the poisons most frequently used, prescribed drugs, may give no proof of the deceased's intent. One would, however, expect to find some difference in the type of poisons employed in deaths classed as suicide and those classed as accidents, if a valid difference between them really exists. Accidental poisonings, by definition, involve random encounters with the wide array of lethal substances found in the home and the workplace. Suicidal poisonings, which involve deliberate encounters with the poison, would be expected to favour the least unpleasant toxic substances available and especially, since psychiatric illness is such a common precursor of suicide, the psychotropic drugs. The distribution of substances responsible for poisoning deaths given open verdicts should, on this reasoning, lie somewhere between those for suicides and for accidents.

To test this hypothesis, poisoning statistics for 1968–70 were examined (Barraclough, 1974a). In this 3-year period there were 8,635 poisoning deaths of which 65 per cent were classed as suicides, 17 per cent as accidents and 18 per cent as undetermined. The substances causing death were divided into 27 groups using ICD N codes. The rank order of the percentage distribution of substance groups was found to be almost the same for all three classes of death. Further, barbiturates accounted for 67 per cent of suicides, 69 per cent of undetermined deaths and 60 per cent of accidents: and all psychotropic drugs combined for 83, 86 and 79 per cent, respectively (Table 5.9).

Table 5.8: Distribution of Verdicts by Coroner's Officer Investigating the Case and Pathologist Conducting the Autopsy The coroner's verdict

Case investigated by	Open verdict (N = 110)		Suicide verdict (N = 110)		Accidental death verdict (N = 110)		Total	
	N	%	N	%	N	%	N	%
Coroner's officer								
1	16	35	17	37	13	28	46	100
2	3	30	1	10	6	60	10	100
3	22	37	19	32	18	31	59	100
4	3	19	6	38	7	44	16	101
5	8	29	9	33	10	37	27	99
6	4	44	1	11	4	44	9	99
7	9	39	9	39	5	22	23	100
8	4	33	6	50	2	17	12	100
9	4	40	5	50	1	10	10	100
10	13	30	15	35	15	35	43	100
11	7	37	6	32	6	32	19	101
12	7	50	3	21	4	29	14	100
13	10	27	11	29	16	43	37	99
14	0	0	2	40	3	60	5	100
	110		110		110		330	

$\chi^2 = 21.27$; d.f. $= 26$; $p < 0.80$.

Table 5.8: *Continued*

The coroner's verdict

Autopsy conducted by	Open verdict		Suicide verdict		Accidental death verdict		Total	
	N	%	N	%	N	%	N	%
Pathologist								
1	10	53	6	32	3	16	19	101
2	11	37	10	33	9	30	30	100
3	20	37	23	43	11	20	54	100
4	59	30	61	31	74	38	194	99
5	10	30	10	30	13	39	33	99
	110		110		110		330	

$\chi^2 = 11.05$; d.f. = 8; $p < 0.20$.
Source: Barraclough *et al.* (1976).

The result suggests that the coroner's definition cannot distinguish between the suicide and the accident in poisoning from psychotropic drugs. The fact that four out of five accidental and undetermined death poisonings are from psychotropic drugs has led some, including the Registrar General's office, to conclude that all poisonings are in fact suicides, and to

Table 5.9: Coroners Verdicts for Poisoning Deaths 1968–1970

Substance	Suicide (N = 5,637)	Undetermined (N = 1,547)	Accident (N = 1,451)
	%	%	%
Barbiturates	70.01	71.76	63.20
Analgesics, Non-opiate	10.24	7.43	5.31
Antidepressants	4.19	4.65	4.55
Methaqualone	3.76	2.19	3.65
Other sedatives and hypnotics	2.32	3.17	2.55
Tranquillisers	1.84	2.26	3.24
Corrosives	1.65	0.78	0.69
Cyanide	1.35	0.45	0.21
Phenothiazines	1.31	2.19	1.86
Other substances	1.13	1.49	2.33
Opiates and synthetic analogues	0.69	0.52	2.48
Agents affecting autonomic nervous system	0.62	0.84	1.24
Agents affecting cardio-vascular system	0.32	0.45	0.34
Anticonvulsants	0.21	0.19	0.14
Metals	0.11	0.12	0.49
Agents affecting musculo-sceletal system	0.09	0.13	0.00
Antidiabetic agents	0.09	0.32	0.28
Amphetamines	0.05	0.06	0.48
Ethyl alcohol	0.04	0.32	5.72
Industrial solvents	0.04	0.19	0.55
Systemic agents	0.04	0.13	0.14
Other alcohols	0.02	0.32	0.55

Source: Barraclough (1974a).

treat them so in official statistics. This conclusion seems premature in the absence of more direct evidence from case studies, a matter considered in more detail in Chapter 6 on undetermined deaths.

CONCLUSIONS

There are large differences between national suicide rates. Ascertainment procedures cannot explain more than a small part of these differences, at least for those states considered here. Genuine international differences in suicide incidence therefore appear to exist, and these provide a 'natural experiment' for studies which aim to determine how disease and environmental factors influence the frequency of suicide.

In England and Wales official suicide statistics result from a highly organised system for notifying, investigating and certifying death, and collecting and analysing data on death returns to the OPCS, with checks and reviews at each step. Error arising from notifying deaths and from the collection and analysis of statistics is probably negligible. Error is more likely to arise from the coroner's decision, but taking the nation as a whole, unevenness of coroners' decisions averages out to give a stable, statistically reliable rate. At the local level, however, coroners' individual idiosyncrasies occasionally give rise to large variations in the suicide rate. The poisoning death is the main contributor to variation, since its classification can be impossible.

These findings do not demonstrate that the suicide rates of all states and communities are accurate. But they do show that the problem of assessing the accuracy and comparability of suicide rates is soluble, using the scientific approach.

115

6

Undetermined, Accidental and Suicidal Deaths

Coroners in England and Wales can bring in a verdict of suicide only in cases where there is strong evidence of suicidal intent. Self-inflicted deaths where proof of intent is lacking are given an open or accidental death verdict.

For convenience, the legal definition of suicide is restated: 'Every act of self-destruction is, in common language, described by the word suicide provided it be the intentional act of a party knowing the probable consequences of what he is about' (Common Bench Reports 1846: quoted in Thurston, 1976). The coroner's handbook at the time of this inquiry, *Jervis on Coroners* (Purchase and Wollaston, 1957) restates this point of view, saying that for suicide 'There should be some actual evidence pointing to the event; the verdict should not rest upon surmise.' Jervis also gives a reasonably operational definition of an accident: 'Accident would presumably be interpreted in the popular sense as meaning an unlooked for mishap or an untoward event which is not expected or designed.' To cope with the unknowable, Jervis explains how the open verdict should be used: 'If there is insufficient evidence to record any of the other suggested verdicts.'

These definitions are more than advice, for they are tested in the higher courts from time to time and reiterated (Jennings and Barraclough, 1980). The contemporary coroner's handbook *Coroners' Inquiries* upholds them (Burton *et al.*, 1985).

The effect of these legal definitions on the classification of violent death, described in the previous chapter, means that deaths with a self-inflicted element given open or accidental death verdicts must be of interest to the student of suicide, and also to the clinician. This chapter summarises inquiries which

116

aimed to describe the clinical and social features of these neglected classes of death, and their relation to suicide.

OPEN VERDICTS

A separate class for the death with a self-inflicted element which was a likely suicide but could not be classified as one because there was no proof of intent, a requirement in many countries, has been recognised by the International Classification of Diseases (ICD) and its predecessors. But the Revisions of this disease classification, published every 10 years or so since the end of the last century, have differed as to whether to classify open verdicts with accidents, with suicides, or to an independent class (Jennings and Barraclough, 1980).

Until the Fourth Revision came into force in 1931, the ICD included open verdicts with accidents. From 1931 to 1939 the ICD had a category (195), similar to the present undetermined death, which included death from violence returned as 'open verdict', 'found drowned', and 'found dead on a railway or shore'. With the Fifth Revision (1940) open verdicts were again included with accidents. The Sixth Revision (1948) included 'non-accidental self-inflicted injuries', presumably the doubtful suicide, with suicide. The Seventh Revision (1955) is less equivocal, and states that suicide is to include 'self-inflicted (non-accidental) injuries unless specified as accidental'. These definitions suggest the ICD in the Sixth and Seventh Revisions intended open verdicts to be included with suicides. But the Registrar General for England and Wales continued to code open verdicts to accident categories, and only suicide verdicts to suicide categories, sensibly ensuring the continuity of the English national suicide statistics. The Eighth Revision (1968) introduced 'injury undetermined as to whether accidentally or purposely inflicted' as a separate class and the Ninth Revision (1977), the one in use now (1987), continues the practice.

Today the open verdict, although comprising mainly the self-inflicted or accidental death, provides a home for any obscure death for which the coroner must decide a verdict (Burton *et al.*, 1985). Deaths given an open verdict are therefore a heterogeneous group which do not have an ICD equivalent and are classified to the ICD by the Registrar General's Office from the facts on the death certificate, supplemented on occasion by

117

UNDETERMINED, ACCIDENTAL AND SUICIDAL DEATHS

inquiries to the coroner. Open verdicts are assigned to 'undetermined death' codes when the alternatives are suicide or accident, otherwise to accident, natural causes, or rarely homicide (Jennings and Barraclough, 1980). The undetermined death, not the open verdict death, is the phenomenon of interest to the student of suicide.

Deaths given open verdicts, and subsequently classified undetermined deaths, are not rare events. Of the 575,194 deaths in 1970, 1,626 (0.28 per cent) were given an open verdict and 1,125 (0.19 per cent) classified as undetermined death. In contrast 3,940 deaths, 0.68 per cent of the whole, received a suicide verdict. For every undetermined death there are three or four suicides. If every undetermined death were to be a misclassified suicide, which is most unlikely, the official suicide rate would underestimate the actual incidence of suicide by some 25 per cent.

ACCIDENTAL DEATH VERDICTS

Deaths are classified accidental only after a coroner's inquest. Some coroners assign the doubtful suicide to accident, judging by poisoning statistics (Barraclough, 1974a). The reason for this is uncertain since the open verdict, which exists to cope with the doubtful case, is respectable and correct, a view which has been upheld in several High Court appeals against a disputed verdict, and is insisted upon by 'Jervis' and by Burton *et al.* (1985). But some coroners seem reluctant to use the open verdict. Perhaps they dislike uncertainty, or avoid it with the deceased's family in mind, believing the open verdict carries some of the stigma of suicide.

Accidents, which account for about 3 per cent of all deaths, result from a remarkable range of chance events. Of the 17,000 accidental deaths in England and Wales in 1970, 40 per cent resulted from transport incidents, 33 per cent from falls, 5 per cent from poisoning which was nearly always with psycho-therapeutic drugs, and the rest from mishaps extending from drowning to lightning. About 10 per cent of accidents, some 1,700 deaths, rather more than the 1,125 undetermined deaths, were from causes where suicide is an alternative. If these 2,825 deaths were all misclassified suicides, which is most unlikely, the official suicide rate would be underestimating the actual incidence of suicide by about 40 per cent.

This approach permits a limit to be placed on the error of the suicide rate. Supposing all the 1,125 undetermined deaths and one-half the 1,700 self-inflicted accidental deaths in 1970 are misclassified suicides. Then the error of the official suicide rate cannot exceed 50 per cent (1975÷3940).

AN INQUEST NOTE STUDY OF UNDETERMINED AND ACCIDENTAL DEATHS

The studies discussed in this chapter endeavoured to investigate the relation between undetermined death on the one hand, and suicide and self-inflicted accidental death on the other, using a case description approach, in effect reanalysing some of the facts available to the coroner. The hypothesis, that undetermined deaths resemble suicides more than accidents, was tested by comparing the three types of death. Their seasonal distribution, data of no use to the coroner when reaching a verdict, was compared using national statistics.

No clinical inquiries have been carried out on those deaths given open verdicts or accidental death verdicts in circumstances where suicide is an alternative. The studies summarised here used coroners' documents to investigate the medical and social features of such deaths, and the extent of their resemblance to suicide. Coroners' notes of evidence are an excellent inexpensive source of facts on which to base inquiries of this kind (Holding and Barraclough, 1978).

We studied deaths occurring between 1 January 1969 and 31 December 1970 in the Inner West London Coronership, which has a population of nearly a million, and comprises West Central London on both sides of the Thames from Westminster to Putney. The data were found in the inquest notes. These notes contain evidence from viewing the scene of death, interviewing relatives, friends, employers and any other relevant witnesses, consulting official documents such as medical, hospital and criminal records, medical reports from attending doctors and a postmortem. This evidence is assembled by the coroner's officer before the inquest and is supplemented by questioning of witnesses by the coroner in court. The coroner's court is inquisitorial and admits hearsay evidence.

119

The information in the notes includes — besides age, sex, marital status, occupation and living circumstances — an account of the period immediately before death, recent events of psychological and social importance, and the salient features of the dead person's present and past medical and psychiatric history. The evidence is completed by a consultant pathologist's report based on the postmortem findings and, in most cases, blood levels of alcohol and drugs.

The coroner's inquiry, which is not intended to cover the dead person's medical history comprehensively, must underestimate illness and especially psychiatric illness. The postmortem in contrast may reveal unsuspected disease.

Each set of inquest notes was reviewed and the relevant facts recorded in coded sheets. Some judgements were needed — for example whether the dead person had suffered from mental illness. If a diagnosis of mental illness had already been made in a medical report to the coroner, this was accepted. In other cases the diagnosis of mental illness was reached by the investigators, who were both psychiatrists, on the basis of symptoms and signs present before death, and reports of impaired social functioning. For some there was evidence of mental illness but insufficient to decide definitely, and these were classed as undiagnosable. Independent coding of a sample of cases demonstrated satisfactory inter-rater reliability between the two investigators.

Undetermined deaths

Of the 134 open verdicts returned between 1 January 1969 and 31 December 1970, 110 (60 men and 50 women) were classified to the ICD class of undetermined death. Poisoning by drugs was the most common cause of death (77 cases), followed by drowning (20 cases) (Holding and Barraclough, 1975).

No person seemed to be mentally fit, while 80 of the 110 had a definite mental illness and 30 were probably mentally ill (Holding and Barraclough, 1975). The range of diagnoses is shown in Table 6.1.

There was much evidence of treatment for mental illness both past and present. Forty-six of the 110 had a history of past psychiatric treatment, 26 had attempted suicide in the past, 64 had recent prescriptions for psychotropic drugs and 24 had

Table 6.1: Clinical and Social Features of 110 Undetermined, 110 Suicidal and 110 Accidental Deaths

	Undetermined		Suicide		Accident	
Single	41		27		40	
Married	39		48		44	
Widowed	8		10		7	
Divorced	8		6		3	
Not known	14		19		16	
Total mentally ill	80	(73)	96	(87)	66	(60)
Mentally fit	0	(0)	2	(2)	20	(18)
Undiagnosable	30	(27)	12	(11)	24	(22)
Depression	43	(54)	73	(76)	27	(41)
Schizophrenia	11	(14)	10	(10)	0	(0)
Alcoholism	9	(11)	1	(1)	17	(26)
Drug dependence	5	(6)	3	(3)	11	(17)
Abnormal personality	2	(2)	8	(8)	7	(11)
Subnormal	2	(2)	0	(0)	0	(0)
Miscellaneous	8	(10)	1	(1)	4	(6)
Total mentally ill	80	(100)	96	(100)	66	(100)
Psychiatric treatment	46	(42)	65	(59)	31	(28)
Psychiatric admission	36	(33)	51	(46)	22	(20)
Suicide attempt	26	(24)	40	(36)	26	(24)
Physical illness	41	(37)	35	(32)	62	(56)
Family doctor	28	(25)	32	(29)	54	(49)
Psychiatrist	29	(26)	30	(27)	8	(7)
Untreated	9	(8)	9	(8)	19	(17)
Not known	44	(40)	39	(35)	29	(26)
Suicide note	2		42		2	
Threat of suicide	9		17		3	
Suicidal thoughts	15		17		3	

Source: Holding and Barraclough (1978).

some psychiatric inpatient care in the year before they died. Epilepsy affected ten people, a prevalence 40 times higher than that found in the general population. Postmortem blood alcohol levels over 80 mg% were found in 22 (Table 6.1).

To give some idea of the range and severity of the mental illnesses, and to allow the reader to judge the difficulty of deciding a verdict, eight case histories are summarised.

Depression

An unmarried woman aged 37 was found fully clothed drowned in the Thames. There had been six suicide attempts

121

before, five drug overdoses and a jump into the Thames. She was known to have a manic-depressive psychosis, for which she had received psychiatric care in the past, and at the time of her death was being treated with ECT and tranquillisers as an inpatient of a psychiatric hospital.

Schizophrenia

A bachelor, aged 46, a mental hospital inpatient, had an 8-year history of paranoid schizophrenia, having been at various times disturbed, deluded and violent, requiring treatment with neuroleptics and ECT. His final admission followed transfer from prison. He absconded and the next day walked into a casualty department saying he had taken 100 compound codeine tablets and did not want to live. The next day he died.

Alcoholism

An unmarried woman, aged 36, with a history of psychiatric treatment for alcoholism, was still drinking heavily during the last week of her life. On the night before dying she had a drunken quarrel with the man she lived with, and the following morning was dead from an overdose of amylobarbitone. Threats of self-harm had often been made and she had been in hospital 2 years earlier because of a suicide attempt. Postmortem showed fatty infiltration of the heart and liver due to alcoholism.

Drug dependence

A 20-year-old bachelor was found dead with a full syringe at his feet and a tourniquet around his arm. He was known to inject both morphine and barbiturate intravenously and to have been a psychiatric day hospital patient, unsuccessfully, 2 years before. A month before death he was charged with possessing dangerous drugs and was depressed, fearing a prison sentence. He had threatened suicide and inquired about the size of a fatal dose of barbiturate. The night before his court appearance was spent with his girl friend, herself a registered addict. She said he 'fixed' the contents of 35 capsules of sodium amylobarbitone and drank beer and whisky. Death was caused by alcohol and barbiturate poisoning.

Abnormal personality

A bachelor of 23, described by his psychiatrist as a psychopath, was being treated as an outpatient with twice-weekly injections of fluphenazine enanthate. He had frequent bouts of depression, during which he would mention suicide. Over the previous 5 years numerous hospital admissions had been required. He had attempted suicide four times, by poisoning on three occasions and once by gassing. Death resulted from a barbiturate overdose.

Subnormality

A bachelor aged 44 was found fully clothed drowned in the Thames. He had lived in a mental handicap hospital for 30 years, being unable to support himself. He could, however, spend weekends with his family, finding his own way, and it was on one of these weekends that he drowned, in unknown circumstances.

Other diagnoses

A housewife, aged 50, was found at home exsanguinated, having opened blood vessels in her wrists with her husband's razor. She had slashed her wrists on two other occasions, acts not regarded as serious suicide attempts. Five years before death she had recovered from a menopausal depression. Three years before death she was successfully treated for alcoholism with psychotherapy, and for the last 8 months had treatment for agoraphobia with an antidepressant. Death resulted from the haemorrhage together with alcohol and barbiturate poisoning.

An unmarried woman aged 41 was found dead in a hotel room from self-poisoning with amitriptyline, an antidepressant drug, and alcohol. The police knew her as a local drunk of no fixed abode. A close friend said she drank heavily and had an unsettled personality. Shortly before death she had become quiet and withdrawn, saying she had cancer or TB. She was worried about recent trouble with the law and failure to find permanent accommodation. There was no history of psychiatric treatment nor postmortem evidence of alcohol-related disease, so she was given a tentative diagnosis of depression and alcoholism.

Conclusion

The most important finding is the high prevalence of mental illness, especially mood disorder, schizophrenia, alcoholism and epilepsy, in a frequency distribution resembling that for suicide (Table 6.1).

A reading of the case histories suggests the most likely verdict for these deaths was suicide. The coroner himself said privately he thought 90 per cent of the 110 were suicides but without enough evidence for a formal verdict. This opinion will be put to the test statistically towards the end of the chapter.

Accidental deaths

The 110 accidental deaths considered here were selected to match the 110 undetermined deaths discussed above for age, sex and cause of death. Matching for cause of death was necessary because two-thirds of the accidental deaths recorded during the study period were, as one might expect, from road traffic accidents, fires or falls in the home, and suicide was unlikely to have explained them. The causes of death in the 110 accidents selected, all potentially self-inflicted, are poisoning by medicines (73 per cent), solitary drowning (12 per cent), falls outside the home (12 per cent) and hanging (2 per cent) (Holding and Barraclough, 1977).

Sixty per cent of these dead people were considered to have been mentally ill, 22 per cent of uncertain mental health and 18 per cent apparently in sound mental health at the time of death. The frequency distribution of diagnoses described in Table 6.1 differs from that for undetermined death; alcoholism, drug dependence and sexual deviation are conspicuous diagnoses but there are no schizophrenias.

Like the undetermined deaths, the accidental deaths had much evidence of treatment for mental illness, both past and present. Thirty-one of the 110 had a history of past psychiatric treatment, 26 had attempted suicide before, 68 had recent prescriptions for psychotropic drugs.

Alcohol had clearly played an important part in these fatalities. Postmortem blood alcohol levels were over 80 mg% in 43 cases and over 200 mg% in 16. Fifty-two (65 per cent) of the poisoning deaths had been drinking before death and 36 of these had blood alcohol levels over 80 mg%. Alcohol played a part in five of the drownings and four of the fatal falls. These findings are emphasised because the taking of alcohol influences the verdict; intoxication impairs intent in the legal sense.

To give some idea of the range and severity of the mental illnesses present, and to allow the reader to judge the contribution of illness to the death and the difficulty of deciding the verdict, eleven case histories are summarised.

Depression

A schoolmaster of 29, separated from his wife and children, died from an overdose of amylobarbitone taken with alcohol. A year before his death, a psychiatrist who saw him after an episode of self-poisoning had diagnosed reactive depression. His family doctor then treated him with an antidepressant and amylobarbitone because he was again depressed, tearful, sleeping poorly and worrying over his impending divorce. Autopsy revealed areas of cystic degeneration in the left frontal, parietal and temporal lobes of his brain, probably the result of a head injury sustained in a car accident 8 years before, after which his personality changed.

An unmarried woman of 41 died from self-administered Mandrax and barbiturate poisoning. Her depressive illness, which had begun after her mother's death, was being treated at the time of her own death with imipramine and chlorpromazine while she was an inpatient of a mental hospital. She took too many sedative drugs, especially barbiturates, sometimes illicitly obtained, and had poisoned herself with them many times before the fatal overdose, which she surprisingly denied taking.

Alcoholism

A 50-year-old company director, separated from his wife for 2 months, died from barbiturate and alcohol poisoning. For 14 years, during which several episodes of delirium tremens had occurred, he had been in hospital many times for the treatment of relapsing alcoholism. The barbiturate, prescribed by his family doctor, had been used in a self-poisoning episode only a week before the fatal overdose.

A housewife of 55, who had spent the year before her death

in a mental hospital because of alcoholism, died from an overdose of barbiturate taken with alcohol. A heavy drinker for 30 years, her addiction was such that 'she would do anything to get money for drink'. The family doctor prescribed barbiturates and anticonvulsants for grand mal fits, the presumed result of alcoholism. The postmortem found a partial gastrectomy and fatty degeneration of the liver, both the result of too much alcohol.

Sexual deviation

A kitchen porter, a bachelor in late middle age who lived alone, was found dead in his room naked, hanging by a rope around his neck fixed to the ceiling, with pictures of nude women on the floor. He was assumed to have slipped off a pile of cardboard boxes heaped as a step-ladder. No history of psychiatric symptoms or psychiatric care was known.

A 32-year-old bachelor, a cashier, was found dead in his room from barbiturate and alcohol poisoning. He had put a note on the door asking to be left undisturbed. Barbiturate overdoses had occurred three times before. Described as a 'very moody' person, he drank heavily but not enough to be called alcoholic. Psychiatric day care had failed to improve him lastingly. He had a conviction for sexual assault on a young boy.

Drug dependence

A housewife of 43, separated from her husband and having outpatient treatment for barbiturate dependence, was found dead in bed from an overdose of barbiturate. Although 4 years earlier she had been in hospital for depression, her psychiatrist reported no recent recurrence of this. She had attempted suicide in the past.

An unemployed warehouseman of 21, addicted to narcotics and methedrine, took too much morphine and barbiturate, in a public lavatory, and died. This took place a week after completing a prison sentence for illegal possession. A previous offence resulted in 2 years' probation with a condition of treatment by methadone substitution.

Other diagnoses

An unmarried nurse of 32 died from barbiturate poisoning. A psychiatrist who treated her for 2 years, both as inpatient and outpatient, diagnosed an unstable personality with dependence on barbiturates and alcohol. In a road traffic accident 7 years before, her spine was injured and she had complained of neck pain and headache ever since. A relative said her personality changed permanently for the worse after the accident. No injuries from this accident were detected at autopsy.

Not mentally ill

A 66-year-old woman was found dead in a bath shortly after a large dinner. She had no history of psychiatric disorder, and was free of physical and mental symptoms at the time of death. The pathologist concluded she fainted in the hot bath and drowned.

A 78-year-old spinster died after taking between seven and ten butobarbitone tablets. Her family doctor said she had heart and lung disease and was taking ampicillin for a recent attack of influenza and bronchitis. He had prescribed butobarbitone as a hypnotic for 9 years. In his opinion there had never been any evidence of mental illness. The cause of death was recorded as acute bronchitis accelerated by barbiturate poisoning.

Conclusion

The most important finding, as with undetermined death, is the high prevalence of mental illness, especially mood disorder and drug or alcohol abuse, preceding accidental death. However the distribution of diagnoses is rather different from that for suicide and for undetermined death (Table 6.1).

Alcohol intoxication or risk-taking behaviour, and sometimes both, rather than deliberate self-destructive intent, played a prominent part in the events which led to death, whether or not the subject had been mentally ill, and merit discussion at greater length than for the undetermined deaths.

For the 66 cases thought to be mentally ill, the illness or its treatment was usually linked to the death, and three types of link could be distinguished. In 50 of the 66 cases death was due to self-poisoning with psychotropic drugs, often taken with alcohol. In eleven instances the victim risked life to gratify an unusual desire: nine addicts died following addictive drug misuse, and two sexual deviants hanged themselves in error. For two cases, mental disorder impaired judgement in a dangerous setting: one man fell or jumped from a window during an LSD-induced psychosis, and another, an elderly man in a confusional state, died from an overdose of his hypnotic. For the remaining three cases there was no obvious link between the mental disorder and the death; a transsexual jumped from a blazing building, a depressive in hospital recovering from a myocardial infarction fell inexplicably from an open window near his bed, and a woman drowned in her bath after an apparently therapeutic dose of the hypnotic to which she was addicted.

Accidents are by definition chance events difficult to explain. This inquiry shows mental illness, because it leads to carelessness and risk-taking, especially with drugs to relieve misery, or less often to enhance a pleasure, is a large part of the explanation. Accidental death contributes substantially to the excess mortality of the mentally ill.

Are undetermined deaths accidents or suicides?

If undetermined deaths are mostly concealed suicides, their characteristics should be those of suicidal deaths rather than those of accidental deaths. To test this hypothesis, the 110 undetermined deaths were compared with the 110 accidental deaths described above, and with a sample of 110 suicides. The suicides were matched for age, sex and cause of death with the undetermined deaths, as the accidental deaths had been.

The findings are described under six headings: evidence available to the coroner, social and demographic variables, psychiatric illness, physical illness, evidence of intent to commit suicide, and circumstances at the time of death (Holding and Barraclough, 1978).

Evidence available to the coroner

The number of informants making statements and giving

evidence at the inquest did not differ between the samples. There was no evidence on the measures used that undetermined deaths had been decided because of too few facts.

Social and demographic variables

No statistically significant difference in marital status was found between the three groups. On measures of social class, undetermined deaths resembled accidents more closely than suicides. Accidents had the most in social classes 1 and 2 (39 per cent), and suicides the fewest (19 per cent), a finding in support of the opinion that the middle classes are given the less stigmatising verdict. On measures of employment and household composition, undetermined deaths resembled suicides more closely than accidents. Accidents had the most who were economically active (67 per cent), and suicides fewest (47 per cent). The effect of mental illness on work ability probably explains this finding. One third of each group lived alone, marital breakdown being the commonest cause of one-person households. Accidents had the most living in private households (85 per cent), undetermined deaths the most in institutions (20 per cent).

Psychiatric illness

Suicides had most evidence of psychiatric disorder, both in the past and at the time of death, while accidents had the least (Table 6.1). In all three groups, psychiatric disorder was common and played an important part in determining death. The frequency distribution of diagnoses showed undetermined death to resemble suicide more than accident. Both suicide and undetermined death had high proportions of depressions and schizophrenias compared with accidents. Accidents, in contrast, had more alcohol and hard drug addicts.

Physical illness

Undetermined deaths resembled suicides for the prevalence and severity of medical illness. Thirty-seven per cent of undetermined deaths, 32 per cent of suicides and 56 per cent of accidents had significant medical illness. There were no cases of cancer; the popular conception that cancer is a common precursor of suicide appears refuted by these findings. The

129

prevalence of epilepsy, present in ten undetermined deaths, three suicides, and two accidents, far exceeds the 0.4 per cent for the general population.

Evidence of intent to commit suicide

Suicides had written notes and spoken of suicide more frequently than the other groups, as would be expected, since evidence of intent determines the suicide verdict. Undetermined deaths were intermediate between suicides and accidents.

Alcohol was detected at postmortem in 36 per cent of undetermined deaths, 22 per cent of suicides and 56 per cent of accidents. Alcohol, since it impairs judgement, may influence the verdict in the direction of accidental death, and prevent a verdict of suicide, since it detracts from evidence of intent. An intoxicated person may be considered legally incapable of planning suicide, or appreciating the consequences of the act which leads to death.

Circumstances at time of death

Undetermined deaths resembled suicides since they were less likely than accidents to have been seen alive in the 24 hours before death, to have had witnesses to the act which caused death, or to have died at home. This finding reflects planning and is therefore evidence of intent.

Conclusion

The undetermined deaths differed, at the 5 per cent level, from the suicides for six of the 23 variables investigated, and from the accidents on twelve of the 23 variables. The undetermined deaths therefore resembled suicides more closely than they resembled accidents, as predicted. However the similarities between undetermined death and accidental death, and the differences between undetermined death and suicide, seem enough to continue the practice of separating undetermined death from the other two. To call a statistic comprising suicide plus undetermined death a more accurate measure of the incidence of suicide than the official suicide rate does not seem correct on this evidence.

SEASONAL VARIATION OF UNDETERMINED DEATHS, SUICIDES AND ACCIDENTS

The suicide rate in temperate climates has a seasonal rhythm with a peak in late spring and early summer. If undetermined deaths are mostly concealed suicides they too should show the same seasonal rhythm. The monthly distribution of undetermined deaths in England and Wales registered between 1 January 1968 and 31 December 1972 was compared to that for suicide, using a statistical model based on harmonic analysis. The expected seasonal variation was found for suicides but not for undetermined deaths (Table 6.2) (Barraclough and White, 1978a).

A similar test was conducted for poisoning deaths. Because these are so difficult to classify many authorities, including the Registrar General's Office, believe all poisonings from psycho-therapeutic drugs, and nearly all the poisonings from non-medical chemicals, are really suicides, however classified. The monthly distribution for England and Wales of undetermined, accidental and suicidal poisonings was compared, applying the harmonic analysis model to the monthly totals of poisoning deaths, for the 7 years 1 January 1968 to 31 December 1974. The expected seasonal variation was again found for suicide but not for undetermined death or accident, which also differed from each other (Table 6.3) (Barraclough and White, 1978b).

These results were unexpected, especially for the poisoning cases, since other evidence has suggested that accidental and especially undetermined poisonings are misclassified suicides. The difference in seasonal variation between the three categories suggests there is a real difference between them, and not one which results from the operation of chance determining the evidence of intent, nor from the idiosyncrasy of coroners. The different frequency of depression among poisoning cases provides a possible explanation. In the clinical inquiry discussed in the first part of this chapter, a diagnosis of depression in the poisoning cases was present in more of the suicides (70 per cent) than of the undetermined deaths (44 per cent) or accidents (31 per cent). The seasonal variation of depression may there-fore explain the seasonal variation of suicide and the lack of a seasonal variation for undetermined and accidental poisonings. If this is so, depressives may be classified as suicides because their method of death is so determined as to leave little doubt about their intentions.

131

Table 6.2: Total Numbers of Suicides and Undetermined Deaths in 1968–72 according to Calendar Month

Diagnosis	Jan.	Feb.	Mar.	Apr.	May	June	July	Aug.	Sept.	Oct.	Nov.	Dec.
Suicide E950–959	1,743	1,533	1,864	1,886	1,960	1,719	1,800	1,606	1,672	1,663	1,660	1,433
Undetermined death E980–989	573	457	539	522	509	493	504	463	497	519	461	465

Source: Barraclough and White (1978a).

Table 6.3: Number of Poisonings Classified to Suicide, Undetermined and Accident in 1968–74, according to Calendar Month

	Jan.	Feb.	Mar.	Apr.	May	June	July	Aug.	Sept.	Oct.	Nov.	Dec.
Suicide E950	1,101	918	1,180	1,162	1,204	1,126	1,151	1,002	1,038	1,018	1,054	933
Undetermined E980	373	288	344	320	338	336	318	319	329	351	310	329
Accident E850–859	271	313	301	273	290	267	304	309	280	295	271	317

Source: Barraclough and White (1978a).

CONCLUSIONS

The high prevalence of psychiatric disorder among those whose death is classified 'undetermined' or 'accidental' shows that they, as well as suicides, must be considered when studying the excessive mortality of mental illness.

Some undetermined deaths are almost certainly suicides which failed to fulfil the legal criteria for a suicide verdict, since they did not leave sufficient evidence to prove their intent. The coroner's opinion, and the accounts of his cases in the clinical study, support this view with some strength. However the absence of a seasonal variation for the national statistics for undetermined death argues against this conclusion being applied to England and Wales as a whole. A resolution of the apparent conflict of evidence could be achieved by a large clinical inquiry based on interviews with relatives. This inquiry could also identify the scope for prevention of undetermined deaths.

Some accidental deaths are also misclassified suicides, but far fewer than for undetermined deaths. The link with mental illness is via the abuse of alcohol, and of drugs, both illicit and prescribed. Prevention here is more likely to result from control of substance abuse.

7

Aftermath of Suicide

Bereavement resulting from suicide, in contrast to bereavement from natural causes, has unique consequences for the surviving relatives for the following reasons. Suicide is usually preceded by a lengthy period, sometimes lasting for years, of disturbed behaviour rather than of normal conduct. This disturbed behaviour results from mental illness, drug or alcohol abuse, or personality disorder. Such behaviour causes grave disruption to marriage and family life, and much emotional distress in spouses and children. There may be loss of income for those in employment. Relatives may even be relieved when burdens of this kind are finally removed, even though the means of removal has been death.

Such relief must be balanced against the negative effects, which make suicide a particularly gruelling form of bereavement. The shock of the event, the trauma of the police inquiry and the inquest, gossip and disapproval among friends and neighbours, publicity in the local newspaper and sometimes radio and television, all add to the relatives' short-term distress. Self-blame for failing to prevent the death, and a sense of stigma, may be longer-lasting. The economic consequences of the loss of a father and breadwinner, and the effect of the permanent absence of mothering and housekeeping, may handicap the children.

The following describes the outcome for the surviving spouses and children of the 100 cases of suicide whose clinical and social characteristics are described in Chapters 1, 2 and 4.

Studies of bereavement by suicide from the United States, as well as case reports and anecdote, emphasise the serious consequences for survivors of suicide, including the possibility of the suicide of the survivor. These reports, based on cases selected because they came for treatment or counselling, or were in some other way unusual, suggest that all those bereaved through suicide have a thoroughly pessimistic outlook. In contrast, the opinions of experienced clinicians in psychiatry, who had on occasion seen the beneficial effects of relief from the burden of coping with the serious mental illness they dealt with, may have developed an unwarrantedly optimistic view of the future for suicide survivors.

Our inquiry is the first based on a consecutive, and therefore unselected, sample of widows, widowers and orphans bereaved by suicide, and for that reason provides a more balanced picture, and one which can be used as a basis for generalisation.

SPOUSES

Forty-four of the suicides had been married, using the criterion that the couple were living together as man and wife within 6 months of the suicide. Only two marriages of the 44 had been judged sound at the first research interview some 5 years before.

All the 44 spouses, 17 men and 27 women, were traced for the purpose of the follow-up inquiry, which took place between 54 and 83 months, with an average of 60 months, after the suicide.

By the time of the interview ten spouses had died. Thirty-one of the 34 spouses still alive were interviewed by a psychiatric social worker using a standard questionnaire. The interview, which also covered the surviving children, usually took rather more than 1 hour. The two spouses too ill to be interviewed, and one who refused to be seen, had most of the facts we required provided by relatives and family doctors. So all cases were traced, and information obtained on those still alive, even though three were not interviewed directly (Shepherd and Barraclough, 1974).

Mortality

The ten deaths, twice as many as would be expected if the 44 widows and widowers had the same life expectation as the general population of southern England of the same sex and age (Table 7.1) suggest that those widowed by suicide have an

135

Table 7.1: Mortality of 44 People Widowed by Suicide

| | Numbers of deaths | | |
	Observed	Expected	p
Average	10	5.3	0.04
Married average	10	4.4	0.02
Widowed average	10	6.3	0.11

excessive mortality, in line with prevailing belief. However the clinical histories, collected at the time of the first inquiry some 5 years before, showed a quite different explanation. Five of the spouses who had died since the suicide occurred had been terminally ill when the suicide took place. Their illnesses almost certainly contributed to the suicide, for example if a sick spouse had been admitted to hospital leaving a mentally ill partner alone, as in the following case:

> A 72-year-old married man with a rather awkward disposition had a 20-year history of recurrent mood disorder, often requiring inpatient psychiatric treatment. His wife had a disabling stroke, his depressive illness recurred and each had to be admitted to a hospital, but not to the same one. The wife did not improve, and went to permanent institutional care. The husband, only partly recovered from his latest episode of depression, was discharged home against his wishes to manage alone, which he had not done before. He hanged himself 3 days later and the wife died shortly afterwards of natural causes.

If these five cases are excluded the number of deaths among the surviving spouses is not excessive, a result giving no support to the notion that being widowed by suicide leads to an increase in mortality for the surviving spouse, the so-called 'broken heart' syndrome. The causes of death for all ten spouses who died, ascertained from their death certificates, were unremarkable when compared with the causes of death for the general population, heart disease being the most common. None committed suicide. This contrasts with a common belief, sometimes stated in texts, that widows of suicides often kill themselves too.

Psychiatric morbidity

One elderly surviving spouse had already been receiving psychiatric care before the suicide, because of dementia, and this continued. Another, a woman in her thirties, had psychotherapy because of boyfriend problems. There were no cases of attempted suicide. These findings show that psychiatric morbidity among the surviving spouses was not excessive, and reinforce the observation that suicide can provide relief.

Personal outcome

We assessed the outcome for those 31 spouses interviewed directly. A global judgement made for each, based on a broad assessment of quality of personal and family life, work and financial circumstances showed 14 to have been rather better off since the suicide, 14 worse off and three intermediate.

Seven surviving spouses had remarried, similar to the number expected from general population statistics. Remarriage was associated with a good outcome: six remarried spouses were judged better off, one intermediate. Certain characteristics of the suicide's clinical history correlated with a good outcome for the spouse: alcoholism, abnormal personality, illness lasting more than 2 years before death, hypochondriacal symptoms, previous suicide attempts and suicide threats. All these factors would have increased the burden for the spouse while the suicide was alive. Outcome was not related to the sex of the survivor, but did have a relationship with age. Younger spouses tended to fare better, partly through successful remarriage: the mean age for the 'better-off' group was 40, and that for the 'worse-off' group 52.

Two case histories illustrate the different outcomes:

A woman of 22 lived with her husband and their two preschoolage children. After the husband had a head injury his personality changed and he became irritable, periodically depressed and violent to his wife and children. A family history of mental illness, for his mother had ECT for depression and his brother drowned in circumstances suspicious of suicide, suggested a genetical tendency to depression and

137

perhaps suicide. Because of the violence the wife went to see a lawyer about a legal separation and came home to find her husband dead from domestic gas poisoning. Despite the first reaction of shock and grief, she recalled subsequently her main reaction to the death was relief. By the time of the follow-up interview, remarried with more friends and training for a profession, she said life was better in every way.

A woman of 50 had been happily married, living with her husband and the youngest of their three children. The husband, previously healthy and well-adjusted, 2 weeks before he killed himself developed a severe depression apparently precipitated by the unexpected death of a colleague at work. At follow-up, the widow said she had never recovered from the shock of the suicide. She had little social life, for her previous leisure had been shared with her husband, and was short of money. She believed her husband's relatives blamed her for his death, and no longer saw them.

Stigma

Though no longer a crime, suicide is regarded by some as a disgrace. The spouses were asked about the attitudes they encountered from others following the death. Thirteen described 'positive' ones such as sympathy, helpfulness and tolerance, and nine described 'negative' ones such as criticism, shock and fear. Nine could not answer the question. Seven felt they themselves had been criticised by others, and there were two extreme cases of this kind. The first was a man who felt he could not return to the town where he had lived with the suicide because of the gossip and blame; the second was a woman with three young children, whose mother refused to help when she was ill and alone because the mother held her responsible for her husband's suicide.

A consequence of stigma might be early move of house, which American investigators had reported in their selected samples. Eight of the 44 spouses moved home within a year of the suicide, a number no more than would be expected when compared to national migration statistics. Those who moved tended to be those who reported negative attitudes from other people, which could be the result of actual criticism or of high sensitivity.

Ten of 29 who had read newspaper reports of the suicide had been distressed by them. Nobody commented favourably on the newspaper report. Even if the style and content had been objectively factual, the spouses felt newspaper reports exposed private problems, and provoked gossip.

No refusal of payment occurred for the 20 cases who had life insurance, though there were delays for four of them and six received only proportional payments (Barraclough and Shepherd, 1977a).

The inquest

The inquest, the modern successor of the medieval trial for self-murder, is a statutory requirement for deaths resulting from suicide, accident, homicide and other unusual causes. Before the inquest, statements from relatives and other witnesses are collected by the police, and a relative, usually the closest relative, has to identify the body. The inquest, held in a court-room and open to the public, is attended by press reporters from the local evening and weekly papers. The events preceding death are established in some detail by the coroner, who checks orally through witnesses' statements while they stand in the witness box. They may be present while other witnesses give evidence, including medical statements and the pathologist's report on the postmortem findings.

Of the 29 surviving spouses interviewed about their experience of the inquest and the police inquiries preceding it, only two spouses criticised the police in any way (Barraclough and Shepherd, 1976b). Most spouses praised the police, considering them kind and helpful beyond their duty. Nearly all who identified the suicide's body were distressed by having to do so and remembered the experience vividly. It is not a legal requirement that this duty be carried out by the spouse.

Though accepting the necessity for an inquest, many spouses found it deeply distressing. The worst aspects included the courtroom atmosphere, which made them feel they were on trial themselves; hearing details of the suicide's life discussed in public, especially when personal information of a painful kind not previously known to the spouse was revealed by others; the presence of reporters from local newspapers; having to wait, without privacy, for long periods; and brusqueness in the coroner's manner.

Two of the 31 spouses believed the verdict of suicide was wrong, asserting the death to be accidental. Only six knew that a coroner's verdict can by appeal be set aside by a higher court with an order for a fresh inquest which may result in a different verdict.

Aid for the survivor

When death results from suicide, the coping of the bereaved is more likely to fail than when death results from natural causes, because the death is usually sudden, unexpected and horrible. The procedure for getting a death certificate, registering the death and arranging the funeral are different, and therefore unfamiliar. The coroner's inquest causes further distress. The survivors may be ashamed of their association with a stigmatised form of death for which they often feel partly responsible.

When interviewing the surviving spouses we made an assessment of the help they remembered receiving, and assessed how far it fell short of a reasonable standard (Shepherd and Barraclough, 1979). Not surprisingly all 31 spouses said they had had needs, classified as shown in Table 7.2. Family members, as expected, were the people most often mentioned as having helped to meet these needs. Clergy were next, followed by friends, social agencies, neighbours, family doctors, solicitors, and 'others' — who included work colleagues, employers, the police, bank managers and, to our surprise, ourselves, the research interviewers who conducted the original inquiry.

Examples of help remembered were the efforts of a health visitor to have a 22-year-old widow released from identifying her husband's body and accompanying her to the mortuary when the law said she had to; and a social security clerk who visited a widow at home, going out of his way to see she had enough money.

The few social workers involved were not always perceived as helpful. One father who asked for help in caring for his two adolescent daughters was offered the opportunity of admitting them to different children's homes in distant parts of the

Table 7.2: Number of Surviving Spouses (n = 31) Receiving Help

Comfort and support	25
Practical help	25
Advice and information	14
Religious counselling	11
Financial help	10
Other	5

country. He refused. Although 13 suicides had either died in hospital or been having hospital outpatient treatment before death, no hospital social worker was involved.

One-third of all spouses' perceived need was completely or partially unmet, and nearly a half had at least one type of unmet need. Two cases illustrate this:

A father of a 3-year-old girl found many practical difficulties looking after her for the 6 months from the suicide of his wife until his mother came to live, especially when the child was ill. He said the health visitor, who came once, advised him, 'You're doing all right. If you can't manage you'll have to park her out with friends.'

A widow with three children, and no money, was refused the Death Grant by the Social Security Office because she and her husband were divorced, although they had continued to live together as a family until his suicide.

The 13 spouses who could not be interviewed because they had died (ten cases) or were too ill or refused (three cases) also had many examples of unmet need, according to reports of their surviving relatives and evidence from medical and other documents:

An elderly man left living alone after his wife's suicide was admitted to hospital 16 months later, chairbound, incontinent, and dirty, with groin dermatitis, varicose ulcers, bed sores and gross leg oedema from heart failure.

Despite these three examples the overall results are reasonably reassuring. The majority of those bereaved by suicide did receive appropriate help, but cases such as the last show that some get left out. Family doctors and clergy, who almost always know about bereaved families, are in the best position to recognise needs and to see that they are dealt with, in the absence of a more organised system.

The unexpected reports of help from the three research interviewers suggest a line of action for the aftercare of those bereaved by suicide. The research interview was not designed to be of assistance, in contrast to the approach of Shneidman and his colleagues in Los Angeles (Shneidman and Farberow, 1961). An attempt at treatment, we believed, would have compromised the interviewers' objectivity and interfered with collecting and recording facts. However, in spite of this effort to be detached, the research interview had been long, sometimes 3 hours, and often emotional for subject and interviewer. The opportunity to discuss the suicide without inhibition and at length with an uninvolved person had been helpful to over half the spouses. The remainder either did not find it so, or were neutral in their appraisal.

Social workers had seldom been working with the families in this sample before or after the suicide. There are several reasons for recommending that social work should be available to spouses and children bereaved by suicide. These include the high frequency of social, emotional, and practical needs among them; the possibility of unhurried discussion about the events leading to the tragedy giving relief; and the high rate of psychiatric morbidity among the children some years later, which might have been prevented. There is a good case for specialist social workers with experience in bereavements from suicide, and possibly other forms of violent death, being attached to the coroner's office.

SURVIVING CHILDREN

The 100 suicides described in Chapter 1 had 45 children under the age of 17. If the sample is typical of suicides in England and Wales, about 2,000 children each year must lose one of their parents as a result of suicide. The true figure is almost certainly higher than this, for our sample of suicides, older than a national sample would have been because the coastal parts of West Sussex are a retirement area, would have fewer young children.

Children bereaved by suicide are in theory subject to the same mix of adverse and beneficial after-effects as are spouses. These effects will be modified depending on the age of the child and the nature of the relationship with the dead parent. Children who were infants at the time of the death, and those who did not live with the suicide because their parents' marriage had broken down, could be less vulnerable.

Children of suicides are subject to additional influences, not present for the spouses, which might lead to a poorer outcome. Years of living in a disturbed home before the suicide, and social and economic deprivation after being orphaned of one parent, could permanently impair normal development. The nature and magnitude of such effects will vary, depending on the sex and stability of the surviving parent, and also whether that parent remarries. Further, some children may become mentally disturbed as they grow older because they have inherited their dead parent's predisposition to mental illness. This genetic influence, although not an effect of the suicide, may be mistaken for one.

The follow-up study (Shepherd and Barraclough, 1976) was based on 36 of the 45 children, the other nine being excluded because they had been under 2 years old at the time of the event, and too young for their response to be ascertained, or because they had been adopted or fostered before the suicide and could not be affected by it. There were 14 boys and 22 girls, the offspring of 5 mothers and 13 fathers who had killed themselves. The greater number of father bereavements is the result of young men having a higher suicide rate than young women. Since more children are bereaved of fathers than of mothers, bereavement from suicide will in general cause more problems from lack of money and other matters linked to fathering than bereavement from conditions where mothers have a higher mortality. There were no double parental suicides, or suicide following the murder of a child or spouse.

The follow-up interviews about the children formed part of the inquiry into the outcome for the spouses, described in the earlier part of this chapter, and were with the surviving parents and not the children themselves, for ethical reasons. We knew at the time of the first interview that many of the children had not been given an explanation of the death, and others knew about it in vague terms only. Direct interviews on a potentially upsetting topic, in a state of such uncertainty and for research not therapeutic purposes, could not have been correct. The material about all 36 children collected at the time of the first interviews, carried out shortly after the suicide, was supplemented by follow-up data gathered 5 years later at the spouse interview. One spouse, the parent of three children, refused to be interviewed, so the facts which required a parental interview apply to 33 of the 36 children in the study population.

Disruption and strain in the family lives of the 36 children even before the parent's suicide occurred may be inferred from a number of observations. Seventeen of the 18 dead parents had been mentally ill when they died, in ten cases for over 2 years, and five parents had shown evidence of abnormal personality also. There had been a marital separation, in which one parent left home, at some time in ten of the 18 families. In one instance the suicide continued to live with his former spouse and children after his divorce from her. Seven parents had been in trouble with the police. Thirteen of the 36 children were not living with both parents at the time of the suicide. Only one child lived in a stable home.

Of the 17 children in the vicinity when the suicide took place, at least six saw their parent's body. For instance a 13-year-old boy had to break into the locked and sealed kitchen where his father lay dead from carbon monoxide poisoning. In other cases the parent who died took steps to protect the children from witnessing the death, for example by sending them to stay with friends or relatives for a few days or by going away themselves. In others, chance determined what the children saw.

Seven children were given no explanation of the death by their surviving parent, eleven received partial accounts which did not include the information that the suicides had killed themselves, and 18 a complete explanation, though it was not always clear if this had been understood. Usually the older children had fuller explanations than the younger. Since children cannot conceptualise suicide adequately until early puberty, and some think death reversible, what they should be told is conjectural.

At follow-up, twelve of the 18 children who had not been told the truth still did not know, according to their parents. This must have been speculation, since the parents could not be certain what the children knew of an undiscussed topic. Many children must have known far more than their parents had told them, because of newspaper reports and gossip.

Twenty of the 36 children lived with their mother alone at follow-up. Fifteen of these 20 had lived with both parents before the suicide. Seven more children had had to try and adjust to a step-parent after the remarriage of their surviving parent. Nine had moved away from home, and in seven of these the departure was premature, not the normal consequence of maturation. The immediate, and the enduring, effect of the suicide on the structure of the family is disruptive.

Ill-effects in the period immediately after the death, such as crying, self-blame, anxiety, clinging, disturbed sleep, and head-banging, affected eight of the 33 children for whom this information was collected. By the time of follow-up 14 children, according to their parent, had developed 'naughty' or 'difficult' behaviour since the suicide, six had had psychotropic drugs from their family doctor or been referred to psychiatrists, and four had been in trouble with the police. In contrast, not one of a comparison group of children of similar age had had psychiatric treatment over an equivalent period of time. The comparison group were the children of the general population subjects used as controls for the original sample of suicides discussed in Chapter 1. These findings indicate a high incidence of psychological and behavioural disturbance among the suicides' children, but one which seemed to decline over time, at least for the less serious conditions.

An assessment of the children's adjustment at the time of the second interview, taking account of health, behaviour, relationship with family members, and school performance, showed 15 to be functioning well, 16 poorly, and five intermediate. Functioning sometimes varied remarkably between siblings.

To illustrate some of these points, and to give some life to the above brief account of shocking experiences, the outcome for two families will be summarised:

The father, a man of abnormal personality who beat his wife, had been an alcoholic for 10 years. Six months before his death he developed a depressive illness. Four months before his death he left home with another woman. She deserted him and he returned home, but his family refused to have him back. That night he drowned himself, a fact the children discovered from newspaper reports. The children continued to live with their mother. She did not remarry, and stayed in the same house and the same job.

The boy, aged 21 at the time of follow-up and 16 at the time of his father's death, gave up his apprenticeship a year after the suicide and drifted into unskilled work, then became unemployed. He broke the law in a minor way, being caught breaking into a pop festival without paying, and took Dexedrine, cannabis and 'purple hearts'. At the time of follow-up he was having psychiatric treatment for depression. He blamed his mother for his father's suicide and said he could not talk to her. His mother described him as withdrawn, morose, and suspicious that people were talking about him.

The girl, aged 20 at the time of follow-up and 15 at the time of her father's death, was well, socially active, successful at teacher training college, and on good terms with her mother. She had never shown signs of adverse reaction.

The difference in outcome for brother and sister is the outstanding feature, and is most readily explicable by the supposition that the boy inherited from his father a tendency to mood disorder, and the girl did not.

The mother had a depressive illness for 2 years before her death and was legally separated, with divorce pending. Her two boys lived with her, and their father visited at least once a week. After arranging for the children to be out of the house, the mother took a fatal overdose. The children then went to live with their father, who remarried 18 months later.

The elder boy, aged 11 at the time of follow-up and 5 at his mother's death, became attention-seeking, slow, difficult, and behind-hand at school at first, but he improved after his father's remarriage and was well and happy at follow-up.

The younger boy, aged 4 at his mother's death and 10 at follow-up, spent 1 day shut in his bedroom after the suicide, but showed no other reaction, and was also well and happy at follow-up.

The elder boy probably had a bereavement reaction, recovering through time and sound parenting. The younger had no observable reaction, perhaps being too young.

146

Conclusion

Adverse effects may have resulted from living with a disturbed parent before the death, the nature of the death, the influence of a single-parent family, or inheritance. There is no way of telling which from this data.

The children had an increased rate of mental ill-health and of delinquency. The tendency had been to improve and most had managed reasonably well, in part due to successful remarriage of the surviving parent and in part because the sick parent was gone. However many children had not yet survived adolescence, a time when, depending how the surviving parent has handled matters, the fact of the suicide could take on a new and possibly pathogenic significance. The genes for mental ill-health could also start to express themselves in adolescence. The handling of children after a suicide seems to be quite uncertain, there being no assured method derived either from science or from tradition. The work of a specialised social worker for widows of suicides, proposed in the previous section, could be extended to include the welfare of the children.

The evidence of stressful life experiences over a sustained period before the death shows that the suicide of a parent is best seen as a major event in an unhappy series and not as an isolated disaster. The outcome results from relief as well as from grief, and on the whole seems better than expected. Had we confined the investigation to the few children showing marked disturbance, the findings would have supported those reporting more severe reactions to parental suicide (Cain and Fast, 1966).

AGAINST SUICIDE INQUESTS

The coroner's inquest for investigating violent deaths is an English institution introduced in medieval times to protect the citizen against the arbitrary justice of the powerful. The original purpose was a public inquiry into suspected murder. Suicide, self-murder in those times, a crime against the self (*felo de se*), was included among the medieval coroner's responsibilities. The inquest, with modifications, has persisted into modern England and been exported to parts of the world formerly governed from London. In some of these countries the

147

coroner's inquest has survived; in others the inquest has been replaced by the medical examiner system which does not require a public inquiry for every case of violent or unusual death.

The scope of the English coroner's work has been adapted to changing times by a series of Parliamentary Acts beginning in the early nineteenth century, part of the sanitation reforms, accompanied by changes in practice as directed or persuaded by the Home Office, the responsible government department. As a result the coroner's responsibility has shifted from crime detection to accuracy of death certification. The Coroner's Rules 1984, which replace the Coroner's Rules 1953, consolidating the amendments of 30 years, emphasise this shift from crime.

The scope of the coroner's influence is considerable. A third of all deaths, some 170,000 per year, are referred to him for advice. Of these, 23,000 go to inquest. Some 6,000 inquests each year are on cases where suicide might have occurred, there are some 400 homicides, and the rest are accidents (Jennings and Barraclough, 1980).

Our clinical research interviews with the relatives of suicides showed that the coroner's inquest in a public courtroom causes distress to many of the survivors; to spouses as described in the earlier part of the chapter, also to parents, adult children and other close relations. This distress seemed unnecessary. A private inquiry would have produced the same result, been less of an ordeal for the relatives, cheaper for the taxpayer, and most important would come to resemble more closely the procedure for certifying death from so-called natural causes, thereby helping to remove the stigma attaching to death from suicide.

As our own clinical research progressed, a Report was published by a Home Office committee investigating the scope for reforming coroners' practice, the 'Brodrick Report' (Home Office, 1971). This Committee was to recommend reforms for Parliament to legislate. The conclusions of the Report, based on the legal administrators' point of view, were interestingly supplemented by an inquiry into the attitudes of relatives who had experienced a coroner's inquest. As part of this inquiry a private survey firm had interviewed the relatives of 56 suicides during the month following the inquest on their dead relative.

The findings from our clinical research interviews, and those of the survey commissioned by the Brodrick Report, had much in common (Barraclough and Shepherd, 1977b). Both surveys reported that the inquest procedure — especially viewing the body, giving evidence in court, and reading newspaper accounts of the inquest — are sources of much distress to surviving relatives.

Is it necessary, therefore, for all suspected cases of suicide to be subjected to an inquest in the present form? The answer to this question may be considered by discussing the long-established purposes of the inquest as set out in the Brodrick Report. They are: determining the medical cause of death, allaying suspicion, publicising a hazard, advancing knowledge, and preserving the rights of interested parties.

Determining the medical cause of death, the most important function of the inquest, is fulfilled by a medical report and the pathologist's postmortem. A public inquiry serves no useful extra purpose.

Allaying suspicions of murder or malpractice do constitute good grounds for a public inquiry, especially for those who die while compulsorily detained in hospital or prison. But these grounds are relevant for a very small number of cases of suspected suicide, as the following evidence shows. One relative in the Brodrick Committee's survey alleged murder, and seven suicides of the 100 in our clinical inquiry had been compulsorily detained under the 1959 Mental Health Act when they died. There were no allegations of medical or administrative malpractice in either inquiry. This apparently benign attitude has shown signs of change more recently, with actions for negligence being sought by relatives of those committing suicide while having psychiatric treatment.

Publicising a hazard is an argument for retaining public inquests for accidents resulting from dangers in the environment, such as faulty appliances or road design, but not for suicide. Drawing attention to a spectacular method of suicide, such as self-immolation, has been shown to be followed by a series of suicides using the same method. Suicide can be contagious, perhaps precipitating deaths that would not otherwise have occurred.

The advancement of knowledge might be prejudiced by a private inquiry. Coroners' inquest notes are a valuable source of facts on which to base scientific investigations. Coroners would refuse to disclose the names and addresses of relatives for interview for research purposes, if the inquest were to be replaced by a private inquiry. They would, however, provide their notes to be inspected by established scientists.

149

The main legal interests of other parties in suicide are challenging a verdict of suicide felt to be objectionable on moral grounds, or because of possible loss of life insurance payments. The procedure for quashing a suicide verdict does not require a public inquiry to have decided the cause of death. Insurance companies act on the death certificate, and deal with suspected fraud by appeals against an accident or open verdict in cases which they think are concealed suicide, or by refusing to pay insurance claims on cases of suicide. Such occurrences are believed to be rare because the suicide clause in life insurance policies for most companies only excludes payment if suicide takes place in the first year of the policy (Barraclough and Shepherd, 1977a). No cases in our clinical study of suicide had life insurance payment refused.

These arguments show that the public inquest is unnecessary for more than 90 per cent of cases of suicide. Our conclusion from the clinical research studies is in accord with the Brodrick Report's recommendation that public inquests should be reserved for those suspected suicides where homicide is a possibility, for unidentified bodies, and for those dying while deprived of liberty. Applying these criteria to our own sample of 100 suicides, only seven would have needed an inquest, all because the deceased had been detained under the Mental Health Act at the time of death.

Reform of the inquest procedure would save money and avoid a great deal of distress to vulnerable people. Further, the stigma attached to suicide is almost certainly maintained by the public nature of the inquiry and the newspaper reporting afterwards. Parliament has never acted on the Brodrick Report's findings. Such is the inertia of a long-established set of procedures which are working tolerably well, from the legal administrator's point of view.

NEWSPAPER REPORTING

The evening newspapers of cities and towns, which specialise in news of local interest, are seen by over 80 per cent of their potential readership in Britain. They publish coroners' court proceedings for three-quarters of suicide cases. The presence of reporters in court, and the subsequent publication of the account of the inquest, sometimes in remarkable detail, were sources of much distress to the relatives in our clinical inquiry and the Brodrick Committee's commissioned survey. Newspaper reports are often biased towards the unusual and sensational. In the newspaper we studied, the Portsmouth *News*, one of the better evening newspapers, suicides using violent methods and the suicides of young people tended to receive prominent displays, large front page headlines and more space, compared with the reporting of the more run-of-the-mill case (Shepherd and Barraclough, 1978). Tragic events affecting ordinary people, a cynical definition of 'news', are used to promote newspaper sales, a practice justified by the newspaper proprietors, who stand to profit, on the grounds of 'public interest'. There is no genuine public interest served by publishing reports of suicide, as can be seen from the arguments set out in the preceding section. And if the newspapers were serving the public interest they would give all cases equal space or print nothing.

Apart from causing distress to relatives, newspaper reports of suicide have been conjectured to prompt other people to kill themselves. William Farr, the first medical statistician to the Registrar General, a man who took an interest in suicide and the waywardness of coroners over a long career, wrote 'A single paragraph may suggest suicide to twenty persons; . . . so the advantages of publicity counterbalance the evils attendant on one such death' (HMSO, 1841).

Newspaper strikes are not associated with reductions in the suicide rate. But increases in suicide following reports of the suicide of a famous person, or suicide by a spectacular method, have often been recorded, suggesting that aberrant behaviour is contagious. In contrast, the effect of the reporting of the 'everyday' suicide in local newspapers on subsequent suicide occurrence had not been investigated until we carried out a study to investigate that possibility.

If newspaper reports incite people to kill themselves, suicides should be preceded by more reports than would be expected by chance. This phenomenon was studied using a local newspaper (Barraclough, Shepherd and Jennings, 1977). Twice the expected number of newspaper reports about suicide were found for the week before death for suicides of men under the age of 44 (Table 7.3). However, the observed and expected numbers of

151

reports were equal for women and for older men. Since there was no clear reason to account for the effect being confined to young men, chance seems as likely an explanation as a causal link. The result is, however, sufficiently clear-cut to suggest there may be a relationship worth pursuing with further inquiries.

Table 7.3: Newspaper Reports about Suicide Preceding the Suicide of 20 Men under 44

	Numbers of newspaper reports		
Days before suicide	Observed	Expected	p
2	8	4.0	0.03
4	13	7.2	0.01
7	16	11.0	0.05

William Farr also wrote (HMSO, 1841) 'Why should cases of suicide be reported at length in public papers any more than cases of fever?' In many countries, including Scotland, suicide is not systematically reported; our studies suggest that it would be better if the English press stopped reporting it also.

CONCLUSIONS

In theory, death from suicide may have both beneficial and deleterious consequences for the survivors. The evidence presented here suggests that, for spouses and for children, outcome in the longer term, though not perhaps the short, tends to be polarised into either favourable or unfavourable; about half the survivors eventually emerging rather better off and about half worse off, with very few in between. The literature reports one other follow-up of spouses bereaved by suicide, with findings in broad agreement (Demi, 1984).

Short-term distress after bereavement by suicide, though to a large extent inevitable, could be reduced if surviving spouses did not have to identify the body themselves or appear at the public inquest, and if reports of such deaths were not published in newspapers. Inquests, and the newspaper reports of them, serve no useful purpose in at least 90 per cent of suspected suicide cases. The abandonment of the coroner's public inquiry for suicide would be no loss. However the Coroner's Rules

1984, which provided an opportunity for reform based on the Brodrick Report's recommendations, state that all inquests must be held in public, except in cases affecting national security.

8

Prevention of Suicide

Spending public funds on research into the causes of suicide has a practical justification if the results lead to effective methods of prevention. From the clinical point of view, approaches to preventing suicide include methods to identify potential suicides and methods to treat them when identified. This chapter describes inquiries about the effectiveness of lay counselling by the Samaritans; the evidence for a medical approach; and the feasibility of limiting the availability of barbiturates, once the most common means of fatal self-poisoning, the lessons from which are still important.

THE SAMARITANS

The Samaritans, a voluntary organisation conceived by the Reverend Chad Varah in 1953, exists to help suicidal and despairing people. Clients usually make their first contact with the service by calling in without appointment or by telephone, often anonymously. They may go on to receive prolonged counselling, known as 'befriending'. Befriending has the aim of providing support, facilitating the kind of personal changes which occur in psychotherapy, or giving practical help in forming social links. Counsellors are taught to recognise and refer mentally ill clients for psychiatric treatment.

From their modest and unique beginning in the crypt of the Lord Mayor's Church of London, the Samaritans expanded on a national and then international scale. By 1975 there were 165 branches in the United Kingdom and Eire, handling a million telephone calls a year. By 1984 there were two million calls a

154

year. Though the scale of this expansion shows the Samaritans fulfil a widespread need for relief of psychological distress, critics have expressed doubt as to whether they attract the suicidal, or achieve their primary aim of preventing the occurrence of suicide by befriending.

Doubt about clients being at high risk of committing suicide is supported by Samaritan statistics which show clients are mainly young, female, and married, whereas suicide occurs more often in older people, among men rather than women, and in those living alone. Because suicide is so often the culmination of intractable mental illness and social disruption, which has continued despite professional efforts, lay counselling seems unlikely to work even if it did reach the right people.

The first of, the studies summarised here (Barraclough and Shea, 1970) was carried out with the collaboration of Miss M. Shea, a Samaritan counsellor able to inspect client files without compromising confidentiality. We aimed to examine the period elapsing between self-referral and death for Samaritan clients who committed suicide, calculate a suicide rate for Samaritan clients, and discover the proportion of all suicides in contact with the Samaritans. We achieved these aims by comparing the coroner's list of names of suicides with the Samaritan client register in each of six large towns in southern England which had active Samaritan branches.

We found 45 suicides who had been Samaritan clients. The suicide occurred within a month of first Samaritan contact for a third of them, and within 2 years for most of the others (Fig. 8.1). Calculations based on these findings (Table 8.1) show a suicide rate of 285 per 100,000 in the first year after contact, one of the highest rates for any defined special group and some 25 times greater than the general population risk.

Some 4 per cent of all the suicides which occurred over the period studied had been known to a Samaritan branch, and sometimes to more than one, a satisfactory result in one sense since it proved the organisation attracted the suicidal.

The high suicide rate for Samaritan clients in the year after referral shows conclusively that the Samaritans do attract suicidal people. However it remains true that over 99 per cent of Samaritan clients do not commit suicide. A second study (Barraclough and Shea, 1972), designed to identify characteristics distinguishing suicidal clients from clients who did not kill

155

Table 8.1: Suicide Rates per 100,000 for Samaritan Clients

	Rate	N
Rate for 1st-year clients	285	26
Rate for 2nd-year clients	125	8
Rate for 3rd-year clients	65	3
Eight-year average rate	119	42
Rate for England and Wales population	15	
Rate for England and Wales population of comparable age and sex	11	

themselves, was undertaken because the results might be of practical value to the Samaritan counsellor faced with the impossible task of identifying the one in every 300 clients who is going to commit suicide. We compared the Samaritan branch's client records for the 45 suicides with those of a control group, 90 randomly selected Samaritan clients who had not killed themselves. Statistical power is increased by doubling the number of controls. We compared the clinical and demographic features of the clients, their treatment and the characteristics of their counsellors.

The treatments given to both suicides and controls were similar, and their counsellors were of comparable sex, age and social background. But male sex, older age, living alone or in non-private accommodation, a disrupted marriage and a past history of attempted suicide were all factors more commonly found in the suicide group than the control. Two features, a history of treatment from a psychiatrist and being involved with medical or non-medical helping bodies at the time of the Samaritan contact, were possessed by 44 of the 45 suicides but only 40 of the 90 controls. These facts were taught to Samaritan counsellors to help them identify clients at high risk for suicide.

The finding that the Samaritans attract the suicidal, although useful to the organisation in one sense, paradoxically cast doubt on their ability to prevent suicide, reinforcing the sceptical opinions of clinicians mentioned earlier.

Between 1963 and 1970 the Samaritan organisation expanded rapidly, and the suicide rate in England fell by a third, from 12 to 8 per 100,000, a fall not paralleled in other European

Figure 8.1: Interval Between Self-referral and Suicide for 45 Samaritan Clients

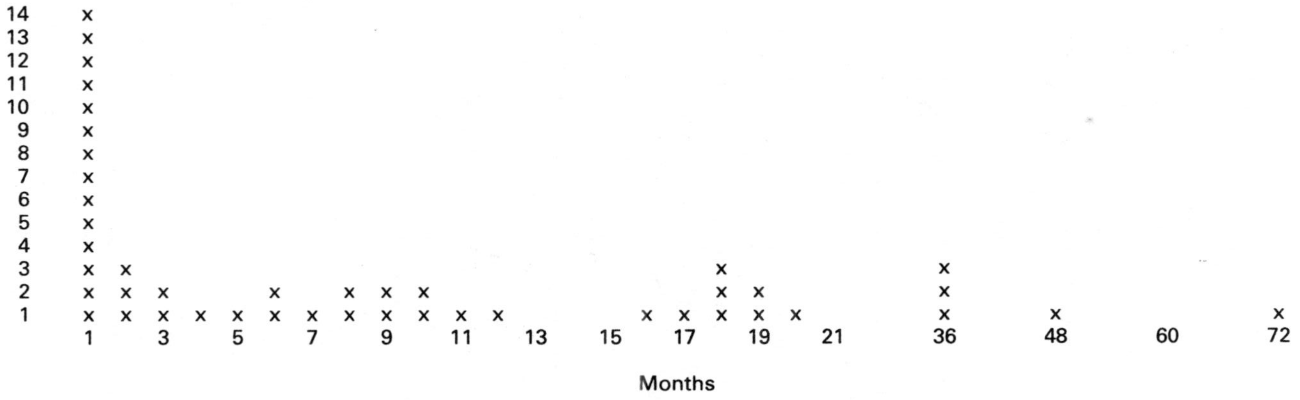

```
14  ×
13  ×
12  ×
11  ×
10  ×
 9  ×
 8  ×
 7  ×
 6  ×
 5  ×
 4  ×
 3  ×  ×                 ×
 2  ×  ×  ×  ×  ×         ×  ×                    ×
 1  ×  ×  ×  ×  ×  ×  ×   ×  ×  ×                 ×        ×
    1  3  5  7  9  11 13  15 17 19 21            36       48       60       72
```

Months

countries. The conjectured explanations for this fall included the substitution of methane for carbon monoxide in the domestic gas supply, improved hospital care of the poisoned, better treatment of depressed patients by general practitioners, improvements in psychiatric services, affluence, high employment, and the Samaritans. Some of the Samaritans' supporters pointed to the fall in the suicide rate as proof of the effectiveness of their work. A study (Bagley, 1968) showing the suicide rate fell by 6 per cent in 15 towns with a Samaritan branch, but rose by 20 per cent in 15 matched control towns without one, supported this claim.

My research experience, interviewing relatives of suicides, had made me doubt the Samaritans' ability to prevent suicide. So, when enough time had elapsed for a longer experience of the Samaritans' services, we repeated Bagley's inquiry using a larger number of towns and better methods for selecting 'control' towns (Barraclough, Jennings and Moss, 1977: Jennings, Barraclough and Moss, 1978). For 33 towns which had Samaritan branches, we used four separate sets of criteria to select control towns without branches. The control was the town closest to the Samaritan town on each measure at the time the branch opened.

None of the four comparisons showed a significant difference between Samaritan and control towns on the measure used, the mean percentage change of the suicide rates of Samaritan towns and control towns before and after the opening of the Samaritan branch (Table 8.2). The suicide rates of Samaritan towns and their controls declined together, and are not distinguishable (Fig. 8.2).

These results are not compatible with the Samaritans making a substantial contribution to preventing suicide, however valuable their work may be in providing comfort and relieving distress. The decline of the English suicide rate did not continue after 1970, despite the continued increase of Samaritan activities, and now in the 1980s the suicide rate is rising.

The apparent success of the Samaritans has been cited in support of similar organisations, especially in the United States of America where telephone counselling had received Federal funding; it has brought the Samaritans much public support, and attracted a great deal of interest from behavioural scientists

Table 8.2: Mean Percentage Change in Suicide Rates of Samaritan and Control Towns Before and After Opening of a Samaritan Branch

Method of choosing controls	N	Mean percentage change		Wilcoxon test (one-tailed) p
		Samaritan	Control	
I. Matching on four components: Bagley's towns only	15	0.0	−2.6	0.19
II. Matching on four components: towns chosen from all county boroughs	23	−9.2	−9.6	0.42
III. Matching on pre-opening rate	33	3.0	−5.0	0.24
IV. Matching on single-person households	35	−3.5	−2.5	0.23

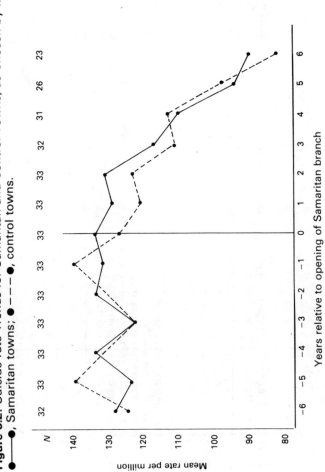

Figure 8.2: Suicide-rate Trends for Samaritan and Control Towns, as Chosen by Method III. ●——●, Samaritan towns; ●– – –●, control towns.

Reproduced with permission of Cambridge University Press, from Jennings, Barraclough and Moss (1978) 'Have the Samaritans lowered the suicide rate? A controlled study', *Psychological Medicine, 8*, 413–22 with a clinical leaning. But convincing evidence that lay telephone counselling prevents suicide has not been found in any part of the world.

A MEDICAL APPROACH TO PREVENTION

Clinical studies of suicides show a high prevalence of mental illness of a kind usually responsive to medical treatment. Further, most suicides have had recent contact with their family doctor, and some with psychiatrists. The data on which these statements are based have been discussed in the early chapters of this book. The medical approach to suicide prevention (Barraclough, 1972c) therefore requires effective treatment of illness without placing lethal supplies of psychotropic drugs in patients' hands.

Treatment of illness

Depressed mood, whether consequent on depressive illness, alcohol or drug addiction, or schizophrenia, has emerged as the most notable precursor of suicide in all clinical studies, whether conducted in England, the United States or Australia. The exceptions are the few patients who kill themselves on the instructions of hallucinatory voices, because of delusions, or because they can no longer tolerate other alien mental experiences. Whether the same is true for non-Western cultures is unknown. Elevation of depressed mood is therefore a prime goal of suicide prevention, but insufficient medical effort had been directed to this end for the suicides in our clinical study (Barraclough *et al.*, 1974). Tricyclic antidepressants were not being used when they should have been and, when they were, doses were too low, or the patient was known not to be taking the drug. Electroconvulsive treatment was underused. In a few cases leucotomy might have been considered.

Between 1966 and 1968, when our inquiry was carried out, lithium carbonate had not yet been shown unequivocally to be an effective prophylactic of recurrent affective disorder. Following Coppen's prospective clinical trial of lithium carbonate prophylaxis (Coppen *et al.*, 1971), which showed that lithium is effective in preventing or attenuating depressive episodes in most patients with manic-depressive psychosis, we re-examined the data on these 100 suicides. Twenty-one cases would have fulfilled Coppen's criteria for entry to the trial, and a further 23 cases might also have benefited from lithium therapy since they too had a history of recurrent depression. This observation suggests that correct use of lithium ought to reduce the suicide rate (Barraclough, 1972b). To illustrate the remarkable benefit which lithium can produce at the personal level, a patient with manic-depressive psychosis and a history of serious suicide attempts agreed to have his biography 'ghosted' after lithium treatment had enabled him to leave his chronic ward (Barraclough, 1975) (Appendix 2). He has remained well for 10 years and, despite the penultimate paragraph of his account, married successfully.

However, despite the promise of lithium, there is disappointingly no evidence that suicide has become any less frequent as a result of its use.

Avoidance of risk in treatment

At the time of our clinical inquiry more than half the suicides in England and Wales resulted from poisoning with prescribed drugs. Reflecting national statistics, poisoning with prescribed drugs had been the cause of death for 56 of our 100 cases. Their suicide dates were clustered in the 10 days following their last visit to a doctor, suggesting the medical consultation might have been motivated towards getting the means for suicide, or that the prescription for a lethal number of tablets obtained at the consultation might act as the precipitant for suicide. Discussion with the general practitioners concerned showed these doctors perceived the main treatment priority to be relief of anxiety, agitation and sleeplessness. They did not appreciate that tricyclic antidepressants and phenothiazines can alleviate these symptoms at the same time as gaining control of the primary psychiatric illness which underlies them. Instead, they overprescribed barbiturates and to a lesser extent benzodiazepines. Poor control of anxiety, disruption of the sleep cycle, decline in mental and motor performance, and addiction resulted, adding to the handicap of the mental illness. In a few cases the doctor lost control of prescribing altogether, and the patient obtained prescriptions on demand from the receptionist by telephone, letter or proxy. On occasion patients altered their prescriptions to get larger amounts (Barraclough, Nelson, Bunch and Sainsbury, 1971). Some of these points are illustrated in the following case history:

A married woman of 38 lived in the private hotel where she worked as a waitress. Her husband and four children were separated from her because she was quarrelsome and neglected the children. This behaviour, associated with a phobic anxiety state, began after the birth of her fourth child at the age of 28. To alleviate her symptoms she took large amounts of barbiturate, to which she had become addicted. Her shrewd general practitioner provided, once a week, seven postdated prescriptions, one for each day's supply of sodium amylobarbitone and chlorpromazine, the dose being written in words. By arrangement with the doctor the same chemist dispensed the prescriptions. A locum tenens wrote the final prescription with the dose in arabic numerals. The patient added a 0, went to a different chemist, got ten times the daily dose of tablets and killed herself with them.

These local findings reflected the colossal abuse of barbiturates which, condoned by general practitioners, occurred on a national scale in the late 1960s and early 1970s. The beginnings of this epidemic can be seen in the poisoning mortality statistics for the late thirties. By 1970 two-thirds of all fatal poisonings, some 2,000 deaths, were due to barbiturates. To test the

Table 8.3: Poisoning Deaths from Barbiturate or Nitrazepam per Million Prescriptions (1965–70)

	Rate per million prescriptions	No. of deaths
All barbiturates	133	12,354
Nitrazepam	11	90

hypothesis that benzodiazepine hypnotics are safer, the death rate from barbiturates in relation to the number of prescriptions issued was compared with that from nitrazepam (Barraclough, 1974c). The results, as predicted, showed that nitrazepam was a much safer hypnotic (Table 8.3).

By the mid-1970s the dangers of barbiturates had become

163

recognised, to the extent that there was a question of introducing a complete ban on the prescription of these drugs despite their usefulness in certain circumstances. The Campaign on the Use and Restriction of Barbiturates (CURB), a British Medical Association committee set up to persuade doctors to limit barbiturate prescribing voluntarily and so avert a legal restraint, asked the Royal College of Psychiatrists to survey consultant psychiatrists' opinions about the use of barbiturates. Of 217 consultants, a random sample of College members, 98 per cent said they never used barbiturates for sleeplessness or daytime sedation, but 50 per cent thought barbiturates useful for special purposes such as abreaction (Barraclough, 1976b). CURB used this material in their educational literature. Fashion has now swung against barbiturates, so that in the younger doctor's mind they are as dangerous as heroin and cocaine and consequently rarely prescribed.

Effective treatment for the poisoned

The Hill Report (Ministry of Health, 1968) for the Department of Health and Social Security made recommendations about the treatment of the poisoned patient. We examined each of the 56 poisoning cases in our clinical study to see whether there had been avoidable shortcomings in management, using the criteria set out in the Hill Report (Barraclough *et al.*, 1971).

Of the 19 alive when found, in only three was there any evidence that mismanagement after the overdose contributed to the fatal outcome. In one case the general practitioner did not visit immediately after being called, in another the police misdirected the patient to a cottage hospital with no facilities for treating or admitting casualties, and in the third the patient was prematurely discharged from the casualty department of a district hospital after an aspirin overdose and sent to a psychiatric hospital where she died from aspirin poisoning. We concluded that improvement in management of the poisoned patient was unlikely to lower the suicide rate.

CONCLUSIONS

The reduction in the suicide rate between 1963 and 1970 cannot be attributed to the Samaritan organisation. Nor is there any firm evidence that it results from better care of the mentally ill. Improvements in the care of such patients has undoubtedly taken place since 1963. Recognition and treatment of depression in general practice has improved, barbiturate prescribing has reduced, and the widespread introduction of lithium into psychiatric practice has prevented many cases of recurrent affective disorder from relapse. But since 1971 the suicide rate has been rising again, despite these improvements in the care of the mentally ill.

Although improvements in medical practice have not been shown to bear a relationship with trends in the suicide rate, suicide prevention must be a serious goal in psychiatric and general practice, and is justified by an accumulation of evidence that better treatment of the mentally ill should reduce the frequency of suicide among them.

Factors other than changes in medical practice influence the suicide rate, suggesting that a public health approach to suicide prevention might be more successful than a case-finding approach. In 1963 one-third of suicides were from domestic gas poisoning, and the drop in the suicide rate over the next 7 years coincided with the replacement of carbon monoxide with methane in domestic gas which took place at the same time. The change in the rate was equivalent to the proportion of suicides previously caused by carbon monoxide poisoning. This suggests the removal of a physical hazard may influence the person considering suicide.

The influence of measures which affect the minds and behaviour of entire populations is suggested by the reduction in the suicide rates for combatant countries during both World Wars, and the increase in rates at times of economic recession. The future may provide the means for organising society in such a way as to minimise suicide by these broad approaches which impinge on everyone.

9

Summary and Conclusions

Our study of 100 consecutive cases of suicide, carried out through interviewing relatives and other informants and studying documentary evidence, with comparison data from 150 randomly selected age/sex-matched controls, pointed to the overwhelming importance of mental illness as a precursor of suicide. For 93 of the 100 cases there was sound evidence of mental illness present at the time of death. Depression and alcoholism accounted for 85 cases. Most subjects had been in contact with doctors shortly before they died, and were taking psychotropic drugs; however, the type and dosage of these drugs was often not appropriate for their condition, and had provided them with an easy means of overdose. More than half the group had given warnings of their suicidal intentions. These findings suggest that the medical approach to preventing suicide, by more efficient treatment of the mentally ill, should be productive. For further research, more use could be made of the suicide brain as a source of data on the biochemistry of mental illness; though such investigations are often hampered by the absence of accurate data about recent diet, drug ingestion, and the exact circumstances of death, as our study about the difficulty of timing of the suicide act has shown.

Abnormal personality, as well as mental illness, was often described in the suicide cases in our sample. Personality has a large influence on predisposition to suicide and on social circumstances, but is notoriously difficult to quantify, and the problems are magnified if the inquiry is made after the subject has died. Future work could include systematic description after the event, or concentrate on special groups where recordings of personality variables have been made in life.

Social problems were common among our series of suicides. Individual factors, often resulting directly from long-standing mental illness, appeared to be of greater importance than general social trends affecting the community at either local or national level. A large proportion of suicides in our sample lived alone, because they were single, widowed, or had disrupted marriages; many were unemployed or off sick because of their mental state. Especially for single men, the recent death of a parent was often a factor which had disorganised domestic life and precipitated a mood disorder, so leading to suicide. The time chosen for suicide was more often close to the anniversary of a parent's death, and for those over 75 close to the subject's own birthday, than would be expected by chance: the annual recurrence of such dates probably intensifies depressed mood. Other 'life events' as precursors of suicide merit study.

Physical illness, on the basis of our clinical study, is less important than mental illness as a factor leading to suicide. Epilepsy is an exception.

Our inquiry into the aftermath of suicide for surviving spouses showed that equal proportions are better off and worse off 5 years after the event. The younger ones especially had benefited from the relief of the burden of living with a mentally ill or drunken partner, and some had remarried successfully. Others continued to suffer from loneliness and stigma after their bereavement. There was no excess of mortality, if spouses who had already been terminally ill at the time the suicide occurred are left out of the calculation. Nor was there any excess of psychiatric morbidity in the surviving spouses.

For the children orphaned by suicide, psychiatric symptoms and behaviour disturbance were common, and presumably the result of being brought up in disturbed homes before the suicide, the difficulties of living in a one-parent family, or the inheritance of mental illness.

Specialist social workers might help prevent the problems which follow suicide. A clinical trial to assess the efficacy of counselling, and practical aid, for families in this situation should be done.

The coroner's inquest had usually been distressing for the survivors, and we concluded that this public inquiry is an expensive anachronism which serves no useful purpose in the vast majority of suicide cases. Newspaper reports, another source of distress to the survivors, have the additional disadvantage that they may incite others to kill themselves; we found an excess frequency of newspaper reports about suicide in the week preceding the suicides of men under 44. Both public inquests and newspaper reports on suicide should be abolished.

Ascertainment procedures, not real differences in the incidence of suicide, are often claimed as the cause of international variation in suicide rates. The rank order of suicide rates of United States immigrants is the same as the rank order of the suicide rates of their countries of origin. This means the differences between suicide rates for the countries of origin cannot be due to different ascertainment procedures, and must reflect true variation in the incidence of suicide. The same explanation accounts for the rank order of the suicide rate of 22 countries being the same as the rank order of the suicide rate plus the undetermined rate, in which doubtful suicides are usually classified.

The rank order of suicide rates of countries may not be influenced by ascertainment procedures, but the size of the difference in their rates is. The suicide rates of England and Wales, Scotland and Eire are in that order. When undetermined deaths are also taken into account, real differences in incidence of suicide between these countries seem less than official rates indicate, but the order remains unchanged. Variation of incidence of suicide in different parts of the world should be exploited as a tool for investigating the effects of cultural diversity on predisposition to suicide.

The frequency of mental illness among open verdict (undetermined death) and accidental death verdicts, where probable suicides are classified if there is insufficient evidence for a suicide verdict, proved to resemble that for suicides in our case-note study of such deaths. However, the seasonal variation of undetermined and accidental deaths is different from that of suicide, indicating there are genuine differences between them. A clinical inquiry, similar to that for the 100 suicides, would further knowledge in this area. Improvements in the accuracy of defining suicide would be possible through development of a rating scale to measure intent. This approach, unlikely to progress while ascertainment of suicide remains in the legal domain, would ensure comparability between inquiries for research purposes.

The suicide rate for England and Wales results from a highly organised system of notifying, investigating, and certifying death. There is no evidence that High Court judgements on appeals against disputed verdicts, changes in legislation, or changes in Home Office regulations have had any effect on the suicide rate. A change of coroner does not affect the rank order of County Borough suicide rates, and coroners' officers and pathologists have no detectable influence on the frequency of suicide verdicts. Occasionally, idiosyncrasies of coroners result in differences in interpretation of the legal definition of suicide. Poisoning deaths are especially susceptible to error. The rank order of drugs used in poisonings classified as suicide, undetermined and accidental is the same.

The Samaritan organisation claims to prevent suicide. Samaritan clients have a suicide rate over 25 times that of the general population, indicating that the Samaritans do attract the suicidal person. There is no evidence that the Samaritans are able to prevent suicide, since the suicide rate in towns with a Samaritan branch declined at the same rate as that in control towns without a Samaritan branch studied over the same period.

There is no evidence that any measure involving individual care or counselling can reduce a community's suicide rate. The proven influences on national rates are the pervasive ones of war, economic depression and environmental hazards such as coal gas.

This suggests that general measures affecting the public health, more successful than medical treatment in reducing mortality from disease, may also prove more effective than the clinical approach in preventing death from suicide.

Appendix 1

The Questionnaire
used in the
Clinical Study

The aim of the inquiry, to record the clinical and social data which could reliably be collected on all cases, was achieved by interviewing those who seemed to know, and by viewing pertinent documents. The resulting information was used to complete answers to 252 precoded questions covering the medical, psychiatric and social history, including an assessment of the mental state in the period shortly before the suicide.

The following list of the principal headings used in the questionnaire also gives examples of how precoded questions were completed, using material from a selection of cases. A positive coding is marked '#'. One section, the description of the suicide act itself, is set out in detail using material from a single case. The names of persons and hospitals are fictitious.

QUESTIONNAIRE HEADINGS

Biographical and demographic (11 items)

Description of suicide act (17 items)
26. What was the dose of the drug used in the suicide?
      9 × 100 mg caps Tuinal.
      What was the blood level of that drug at post mortem?
      1.1 mg% barbiturate.

Previous attempts at suicide (9 items)
35. Treatment for last attempt?

    1 No medical care
    2 Medical care only
    3 Psychiatric
      consultation #
    4 Psychiatric
      treatment

Admitted with slashed wrist 6 months before suicide. Seen by psychiatrist. Failed outpatient appointment. No follow-up.

170

Psychiatric symptoms (40 items)

40. Did the suicide complain of poor sleep or
was observed to be sleeping badly?

1 Severe #
2 Mild
3 No

Duration: *18 months*
Went to sleep OK. Woke at 3–5am.
Couldn't get off again. Taking 300 mg
butobarb. each night.

60. Did suicide say felt useless or worthless?

1 Yes #
2 No

Said 'I am useless', 'not pulling my weight',
'what use am I?', over past 18 months.

78. Was suicide hallucinated?

1 Yes #
2 No

Abusive voices in second person, 'You are
a slut.'

Alcohol (12 items)

89. Ever arrested because of drinking?

1 Yes #
2 No
3 Not known

Jailed for drunkenness 2 years ago.

Psychiatric treatment (16 items)

114. Was suicide currently attending a
psychiatrist?

1 Yes #
2 No

Name of psychiatrist: *Musselwhite.*
Hospital: *Haven.*
Treatment: *Diazepam and psychotherapy.*
Time between suicide and last
appointment: *21 days.*
Time between suicide and next
appointment: *7 days.*

History of past mental illness (7 items)

130. Had suicide been treated previously by a
psychiatrist for a mental illness?

1 Yes #
2 No
3 Not known

Name of psychiatrist: *Kirk.*
Hospital: *Haven.*
Time since suicide: *5 years.*
Diagnosis: *Recurring depressive illness.*
Treatment: *Phenelzine.*

Physical illness and handicap (6 items)

134. Did suicide have symptoms or illness
receiving medical attention at time
of death?

1 Yes #
2 No
3 Not known

Diagnosis: *Allergic conjunctivitis.*
Symptoms: *Irritation in eyes.*
Treatment: *Hydrocortisone drops.*

171

First-degree relatives: number, age, sex, address, date and cause of death

	Age now	Age at death	Death cause	Residence now	Distance
Mother *Pat Smith*	*n.a.*	*62 (1954)*	*Pneumonia*	*n.a.*	*n.a.*
Father *John Smith*	*75*	*n.a.*	*n.a.*	*Wilmslow*	*231 miles*
Brother *George Smith*	*52*	*n.a.*	*n.a.*	*Manchester*	*241 miles*
Daughter *Sammyjo*	*23*	*n.a.*	*n.a.*	*with suicide*	*n.a.*

Education, work and retirement (19 items)
165. Age at which full-time education finished? *23*
     Quals: MB(Edin.).
168. Economic position of suicide on day last known to be alive?

1 Economically active in full-time work #
2 Economically active in part-time work
3 Economically active off sick

Occupation: *Reg. Med. Pract.*
Industry: *NHS.*
Employment status: *Self-employed.*

4 Economically active unemployed
5 Economically inactive retired
6 Economically inactive student
7 Economically inactive other

178. Age at retirement from full-time lifetime employment?
     59 years (1962).
     Reason for retirement?
     Recurring manic-depressive illness.

Income and money troubles (6 items)
188. Had suicide a court order for non-payment of debt ever?
     Court order to pay HP debt. 3 months before suicide.

1 Yes #
2 No

Living arrangements (6 items)
190. Household size and type on day of suicide?

Who lived there?

Suicide.
23 other patients.
Phoebe Ward.
Haven Hospital.
Time there?
2 years 3 months.

1 One person
  household
2 Two person
  household
3 Three person
  household
4 Institution #
5 Hotel/boarding
  house
6 Other

Integration with family (9 items)
197. Time since suicide saw a first-degree
family member not living in suicide's
household?
1 day.
Son visited.

Illness in first-degree family members (3 items)
213. Was spouse under medical care at
time of suicide?

Diagnosis: *Idiopathic epilepsy, 15 years,*
controlled on phenytoin.
Effect on suicide: *No clear effect.*

1 Yes #
2 No
3 Unmarried
4 Not known

Religious behaviour (5 items)
219. Church attendance?

Attended morning service several
times a week (retired vicar).

1 Weekly or more
  often #
2 Monthly or more
  often
3 Two/three times
  a year
4 Never or social
  only
5 Not known

Membership of clubs, societies, etc. (7 items)
223. Did suicide attend clubs, etc., not work-
related, in 3 months before death?

Belonged to none.

1 Committee
  member
2 Regular attender
3 Occasional
  attender
4 Did not take
  part #

173

Migration (4 items)

226. What was suicide's permanent address one year ago?

    1 Same as now
    2 Different #
    3 Not known

    Moved from? *London.*
    When? *8 months before death.*
    Distance moved? *72 miles.*
    Reason? *Husband retired.*

Bereavement

230. Bereaved in year before suicide?

    1 Yes #
    2 No

    Who? *Mother.*
    When? *6 months before suicide.*
    Effect? *Left living alone.*
           Financial loss.
           Loss of social relationship.

Informants

    Name: *Mrs. B. Smith.*
    Relation: *Sister.*
    Period known: *Lifetime.*
    Frequency seen: *Once a week.*
    Last seen: *2 days before suicide.*
    Interviewed: *21 days after suicide.*

Note

    Copy of suicide note

EXAMPLE OF A COMPLETE SECTION DESCRIBING CIRCUMSTANCES OF SUICIDE

11. Address or place of suicide?
    In bedroom.

    1 Home #
    2 Away from home
    3 At home but not in the house
    4 In hospital

12. Did the suicide say he was going to kill himself or threaten to do so within the year before his death?

    'I wish I could shoot myself.'

    1 Yes #
    2 No
    3 Not known

    Length of time since last statement of this nature:
    Past 3 months.

13. Did he talk to anyone about death, dying or suicide in any other way within the last year?

    'I'd be better off out of my misery.'

    1 Yes #
    2 No
    3 Not known

14. Did any friend or relative take any
direct action to prevent a suicidal act?

1 Yes
2 No #
3 Not known

15. Did any friend or relative do anything
else to help or get help for the suicide
in the month before his death?

Sister tried to get her to see GP.

1 Yes #
2 No.
3 Not known

16. Were advance preparations made?

Appeared impulsive.

1 Yes
2 No #
3 Not known

17. Was the act impulsive or deliberate
in the interviewer's judgement?

1 Impulsive
2 Uncertain #
3 Deliberate

18. Was there a note?

1 Signed note
2 Unsigned note
3 No note #

19. Was alcohol taken in relation to the
suicidal act?

1 Yes
2 No #
3 Not known

21. Day of week act began?

1 Monday
2 Tuesday
3 Wednesday
4 Thursday
5 Friday #
6 Saturday
7 Sunday
8 Not known

Was there any reason for the choice of this day?
None obvious.
Probable time of day act began?
0700–0745.

22. Mode of death?

1 Poisoning by
analgesics and
soporifics #
2 Poisoning by
other solids
and liquids
3 Domestic gases

Pathologist estimate:
56–100 capsules quinalbarb.

Blood level: 9.9 mg/100 ml.

4 Hanging and strangulation
5 Drowning
6 Firearms and explosives
7 Cutting and piercing instruments
8 Jumping from high places
9 Other

23. Could any more help have been given by anyone in informant's view?

GP should have been called.

1 Yes #
2 No
3 Not known

24. Could anything more have been done which might have prevented the suicide in the interviewer's opinion?

GP should have been called.
Hospital might have followed up.

1 Yes #
2 No
3 Not known

25. Was the suicide dead when found?

Found unconscious at 0745;
dead when doctor came at 0830.
Time between discovery and admission: *n.a.*
Time between admission and death: *n.a.*

1 Yes
2 No #
3 Not known

26. What was the likelihood of anybody finding out before they were dead that they had taken suicidal action?

1 Very likely
2 Possible
3 Very unlikely #
4 Not known

27. Did the interviewer think the suicide intended to kill himself?

Size of dose indicates so.

1 Yes #
2 Possibly
3 No
4 Not known

Appendix 2

Lithium Carbonate: a Patient's View

I have recently recovered from a manic-depressive psychosis which incapacitated me for 10 years. The agent which effected this change appears to be lithium carbonate. I thought it would be of interest to doctors to know the story of my illness and how my life has been transformed since I started this drug. Perhaps I should start at the beginning.

I was the only son of a post office official and brought up in happy surroundings. I was educated at a public school and spent the war in the army, rising to the rank of sergeant. After the war I joined the staff of a gas company, working as a salesman, and continued in this capacity up to the time of my first illness which occurred in 1954 when I was 30 years old. For a year I was unable to work and was thought to be having a nervous breakdown. I received no specific treatment and think in retrospect this was my first attack of depression. I recovered completely and continued working satisfactorily until the second episode of depression which began in 1961 when I was 38.

For the next 10 years I was almost disabled by alternating attacks of depression and elation, termed mania. The depression was so severe I was unable to earn my living or live independently. All I could manage was to live in protected surroundings, usually a mental hospital. I found that my sleep was affected, as was my appetite, my interest in things, my energy and my sociability. I had uncontrollable fits of weeping and was unable to direct my life usefully. The most frightening experiences were suicidal thoughts which insistently pressed themselves on my mind; they would arrive out of the blue and it took a lot of willpower to resist them. On two occasions I gave way and decided I would be better dead. On one occasion I crawled out along the Tamar Bridge intending to jump, but was rescued. On another occasion I took a large overdose of barbiturates but failed to kill myself. Whenever I was depressed, suicidal thoughts plagued me. It was remarkable how they came and went as my mood changed from depression to normality or elation. However, at least when depressed I was inactive. When manic, which I was on many occasions, my judgement seemed suspended and I did extraordinary things which harmed myself and those around me.

177

On one occasion I was convinced I had a special message which I must give to the Pope to bring peace to the world. In this state of mind I discharged myself from the hospital, withdrew all the money I had from the bank and bought a first class air ticket to Rome. It was only as I reached the Vatican door that sense returned and I immediately returned home again and became depressed.

On another occasion during an attack of mania I bought a garage and a small fleet of cars with the intention of setting up a prosperous business. I knew nothing about cars or running a business and I lost many hundreds of pounds.

These are just two of the more bizarre episodes, but there were many others during which I felt a tremendous sense of well-being, was extremely active socially, extravagant with money and offended people with my outspokenness. In this state I was dragging out my existence as a chronic patient in a mental hospital, having been unaffected in any lasting way by any of the recognised treatments for my mental disorder. As far as I know all antidepressants, phenothiazines, tranquillisers and ECT had been tried. ECT certainly relieved depression, but could not do so permanently and with each recurrence I became more despairing.

Finally a determined effort was made by getting me a hospital job as a porter with easy hours. I was able to live in, a close eye could be kept on me and I was supported by frequent psychotherapeutic discussions with a doctor, and a social worker who gave me constant attention. My employers were tolerant and overlooked many lapses of attendance caused by fits of depression and lack of energy which prevented me from getting out of bed. During a period of 6 months I was off work at least 1 day each week and often 2 or 3. At that time my family life was upsetting, for my aged mother was dying and I thought to myself that when she died there would be nothing left for me to live for and I would probably kill myself. It was while I was in this state that lithium carbonate treatment was started.

Since beginning lithium, with its regular supervision by blood tests, my life has been completely changed. I have not had a day off work since I began taking it, and although I still get fits of depression and elation they are well within my conscious control. I have worked continuously throughout this period and now live an independent existence in lodgings, although I still work as a hospital porter. My sunny temperament, and desire for social contacts, and my outward-looking disposition have all returned and I have a great interest in and enjoyment of life. During the 18 months that I have been taking the drug my mother died and I coped perfectly well with all the difficulties that this entailed, including the management of her estate. This left me with sufficient money to take 6 weeks' holiday in New Zealand on my own, which I regarded as something of a challenge.

One particular feature which is worth mentioning is that I am a single man and I expect I always shall be. There is no doubt that my feelings about women are unusual and have something to do with my wish to continue an independent existence, but I feel that this is nothing to do with my illness; although no doubt it is important in influencing my domestic situation, when I am ill. However, I mention this point because I feel that it has been dwelt on to too great an extent by some psychiatrists in my life, who seem to have sought therein an explanation for all my sufferings. When your doctor thinks things it is very hard for you to resist them, and I feel one could be misled in this way.

No-one can know what I have been through, suffering what must be one of the most terrible afflictions that can occur to anyone. There is always the apprehension, when one is well, that the slightest downturn in mood may herald another bout of absolute despair. I understand that manic-depressive psychosis is a rare condition. Nevertheless this new drug, lithium carbonate, ought to be able to relieve the agonies of at least some of the people who suffer from it.

This account is condensed from an article in *New Behaviour*, 9 October 1975. Since it was written the subject has married successfully. One relapse of his manic-depressive illness occurred after he experimented by stopping lithium.

Appendix 3

The Thirty Life Events on which the 75 Suicides and 150 Controls were Compared, Grouped According to Department of Life Affected

Death: of spouse, parent, sib, child; or household member of other relationship.

Household: change in size or composition, childbirth for subject or spouse, marriage of subject, marriage or preparations for marriage of child, spouse admitted to hospital, other household member admitted to hospital.

Neighbourhood: change of address/hospital/hospital ward.

Work: change of income by a half or more, change of job, stopped work, sacked/redundant, suspended, off sick, retired.

Legal: offences against the law, other legal, involving police or courts.

Medical: admission to general or psychiatric hospital, discharge from general or psychiatric hospital, referred to outpatients.

References

Alderson, M. (1975) 'Relationship Between the Month of Birth and the Month of Death in the Elderly', *British Journal of Preventive & Social Medicine, 29*, 151–6

Alstrom, C.H. (1950) 'A Study of Epilepsy and its Clinical Social and Genetic Aspects', *Acta Psychiatrica et Neurologica Scandinavica. Supplement 63*

Bagley, C. (1968) 'The Evaluation of a Suicide Prevention Scheme by an Ecological Method', *Social Science and Medicine, 2*, 1–14

Bagley, C., Jacobson, S. and Rehin, A. (1976) 'Completed Suicide: a Taxonomic Analysis of Clinical and Social Data', *Psychological Medicine, 6*, 429 38

Barraclough, B.M. (1970) 'The effect that coroners have on the suicide rate and the open verdict rate' in Hare, E. and Wing, J. (eds), *Psychiatric Epidemiology*, Oxford University Press, London, pp. 361–5

—— (1972a) 'Are the Scottish and English Suicide Rates Really Different?', *British Journal of Psychiatry, 120*, 267–73

—— (1972b) 'Suicide Prevention, Recurrent Affective Disorder and Lithium', *British Journal of Psychiatry, 121*, 391–2

—— (1972c) 'A Medical Approach to Suicide Prevention', *Social Science and Medicine, 6*, 661–71

—— (1973) 'Differences between National Suicide Rates', *British Journal of Psychiatry, 122*, 95–6

—— (1974a) 'Poisoning Cases: suicide or accident', *British Journal of Psychiatry, 124*, 526–30

—— (1974b) 'Classifying Poisoning Deaths by Motivation: Anglo-Scottish differences', *Acta Psychiatrica Scandinavica, 50*, 625–35

—— (1974c) 'Are there Safer Hypnotics than Barbiturates?', *The Lancet, i*, 57–8

—— (1975) 'Lithium Carbonate: a patient's experience', *New Behaviour*, 9 October, p. 55

—— (1976a) 'Time of Day Chosen for Suicide', *Psychological Medicine, 6*, 303–5

—— (1976b) 'Barbiturate Prescribing: psychiatrists' views', *British Medical Journal, 2*, 927–8

—— (1978a) 'The Different Incidence of Suicide in Eire and in England and Wales', *British Journal of Psychiatry, 132*, 36–8

—— (1978b) 'Reliability of Violent Death Certification in One Coroner's District', *British Journal of Psychiatry, 132*, 39–41

—— (1987) 'The Suicide Rate of Epilepsy', *Acta Psychiatrica Scandinavica* (in press)

Barraclough, B.M. and Bunch, J. (1973) 'Accuracy of Dating Parent Deaths: recollected dates compared with death certificate dates', *British Journal of Psychiatry, 123*, 573–4

Barraclough, B.M. and Chynoweth, R. (In press) 'Clinical and Social Characteristics of 15 People with Epilepsy who Died by Suicide'
Barraclough, B.M. and Pallis, D.J. (1975) 'Depression Followed by Suicide: a comparison of depressed suicides with living depressives', *Psychological Medicine, 5*, 55–61
Barraclough, B.M. and Shea, M. (1970) 'Suicide and Samaritan Clients', *The Lancet, ii*, 868–70
—— (1972) 'A Comparison between 'Samaritan Suicides' and Living Samaritan Clients', *British Journal of Psychiatry, 120*, 79–84
Barraclough, B.M. and Shepherd, D.M. (1976a) 'Birthday Blues: the association of birthday with self-inflicted death in the elderly', *Acta Psychiatrica Scandinavica, 54*, 146–9
—— (1976b) 'Public Interest: private grief', *British Journal of Psychiatry, 129*, 109–13
—— (1977a) 'Suicide and Life Insurance', *British Medical Journal, ii*, 46
—— (1977b) 'The Immediate and Enduring Effects of the Inquest on Relatives of Suicides', *British Journal of Psychiatry, 131*, 400–4
Barraclough, B.M. and White, S.J. (1978a) 'Monthly Variation of Suicide and Undetermined Death Compared', *British Journal of Psychiatry, 132*, 275–8
—— (1978b) 'Monthly Variation of Suicidal, Accidental and Undetermined Poisoning Deaths'. *British Journal of Psychiatry, 132*, 279–82
Barraclough, B.M., Bunch, J., Nelson, B. and Sainsbury, P. (1974) 'A Hundred Cases of Suicide: clinical aspects', *British Journal of Psychiatry, 125*, 355–73
Barraclough, B.M., Holding, T. and Fayers, P. (1976) 'Influence of Coroners' Officers and Pathologists on Suicide Verdicts', *British Journal of Psychiatry, 128*, 471–4
Barraclough, B.M., Jennings, C. and Moss, J.R. (1977) 'Suicide Prevention by the Samaritans', *The Lancet, ii*, 237–9
Barraclough, B.M., Nelson, B., Bunch, J. and Sainsbury, P. (1971) 'Suicide and Barbiturate Prescribing', *Journal of the Royal College of General Practitioners, 21*, 645–53
Barraclough, B.M., Shepherd, D.M. and Jennings, C. (1977) 'Do Newspaper Reports of Coroners' Inquests Incite People to Commit Suicide?', *British Journal of Psychiatry, 131*, 528–32
Bunch, J.(1972) 'Recent Bereavement in Relation to Suicide', *Journal of Psychosomatic Research, 16*, 361–6
Bunch, J. and Barraclough, B.M. (1971) 'The Influence of Parental Death Anniversaries upon Suicide Dates', *British Journal of Psychiatry, 118*, 621–6
Bunch, J., Barraclough, B.M., Nelson, B. and Sainsbury, P. (1971a) 'Suicide Following Bereavement of Parents', *Social Psychiatry, 6*, 193–9
—— (1971b) 'Early Parental Bereavement and Suicide', *Social Psychiatry, 6*, 200–2
Burton, J.D.K., Chambers, D.R. and Gill, P.S. (1985) *Coroners' Inquiries*, Kluwer Law, London
Cain, A.C. and Fast, I.F. (1966) 'Children's Disturbed Reactions to Parents' Suicide', *American Journal of Orthopsychiatry, 36*, 873–80

Chynoweth, R., Tonge, J.I. and Armstrong, J. (1980) 'Suicide in Brisbane—a retrospective psychosocial study', *Australian and New Zealand Journal of Psychiatry*, *14*, 37–45

Coppen, A., Noguera, R., Bailey, J. *et al.* (1971) 'Prophylactic Lithium in Affective Disorders', *The Lancet*, *ii*, 275–9

Currie, S., Heathfield, K.W.G., Henson, R.A. *et al.* (1972) 'Clinical Course and Prognosis of Temporal Lobe Epilepsy: a survey of 666 patients', *Brain*, *94*, 173–90

Dalby, M.A. (1969) 'Epilepsy and 3 per second Spike Wave Rhythms', *Acta Neurologica Scandinavica*, *45*, Supplement 40

Demi, A.S. (1984) 'Social Adjustment of Widows after Suicidal Death', *Death Education*, *8*, 91–111

Dorpat, T. and Ripley, H.S. (1960) 'A Study of Suicide in the Seattle Area', *Comprehensive Psychiatry*, *1*, 349–59

Dublin, L.T. (1963) *Suicide*, Ronald Press, New York

Durkheim, E. (1897) *Le Suicide*, Paris; translated (1952) as *Suicide: A Study in Sociology*, by J A Spaulding and C. Simpson, Routledge & Kegan Paul, London

Faris, R.E.L. and Dunham, H.W. (1939) *Mental Disorders in Urban Areas*, University of Chicago Press, Chicago

Guze, S.B. and Robins, E. (1970) 'Suicide and Primary Affective Disorder', *British Journal of Psychiatry*, *117*, 437–8

Halbwachs, M. (1930) *Les causes de Suicide*, Felix Alcan, Paris. Also published by Routledge and Kegan Paul (1978)

Hauser, W.A. Annegers, J.F. and Elverback, L.R. (1980) 'Mortality in Patients with Epilepsy', *Epilepsia*, *21*, 399–412

Hawton, K., Fagg, J. and Marsack, P. (1980) 'Association between Epilepsy and Attempted Suicide', *Journal of Neurology, Neurosurgery and Psychiatry*, *43*, 168–70

Henrikson, B., Juul-Jenson, P. and Lund, M. (1970) 'Mortality of epileptics' in Brackenbridge, R.D.C. (ed.), *Life Assurance Medicine*, Pitman, London, pp. 139–48

HMSO (1841) *Third Annual Report of the Registrar General of Births, Deaths and Marriages in England (for 1839–40)*, London

Holding, T.A. and Barraclough, B.M. (1975) 'Psychiatric Morbidity in a Sample of a London Coroner's Open Verdicts', *British Journal of Psychiatry*, *127*, 133–43

—— (1977) 'Psychiatric Morbidity in a Sample of Accidents', *British Journal of Psychiatry*, *130*, 244–52

—— (1978) 'Undetermined Deaths—Suicide or Accident?', *British Journal of Psychiatry*, *13*, 542–9

Home Office (1971) *Report of the Committee on Death Certification and Coroners*, HMSO, London

Jennings, C. and Barraclough, B.M. (1980) 'Legal and Administrative Influences on the English Suicide Rate since 1900', *Psychological Medicine*, *10*, 407–18

Jennings, C., Barraclough, B.M. and Moss, J.R. (1978) 'Have the Samaritans Lowered the Suicide Rate? A controlled study', *Psychological Medicine*, *8*: 413–22

Jones, K. (1965) 'Suicide and the Hospital Service', *British Journal of*

Psychiatry, 111, 625–30

Khron, W. (1963) 'Causes of Death among Epileptics', *Epilepsia, 4*, 315–21

Lindsay, J., Ounstead, C. and Richards, P. (1979) 'Long-term Outcome in Children with Temporal Lobe Seizures. 1: Social outcome and social factors', *Developmental Medicine and Child Neurology, 21*, 285–98

McMahon, B. and Pugh, T.F. (1965) 'Suicide in the Widowed', *American Journal of Epidemiology, 81*, 23–31

Martin, F. (1974) 'Les Epilepsies de l'adulte', *Schweiger Archiv für Neurologie, Neurochirurgie und Psychiatrie, 115*, 209–27

Melville, D.I., Hope, D., Bennison, D. and Barraclough, B. (1985) 'Depression among Men made Involuntarily Redundant', *Psychological Medicine, 15*, 789–93

Ministry of Health (1968) *Hospital Treatment of Acute Poisoning (Hill Report)*, HMSO, London

Morselli, H. (1881) *Suicide*, Kegan Paul, London

Moss, M.L. and Beresford-Davies, E. (1967) *A Survey of Alcoholism in an English County*, Cambridge

Paffenbarger, R.S. and Asnes, D.P. (1965) 'Chronic Disease in Former College Students. III. Precursors of suicide in early and middle life', *American Journal of Public Health, 56*, 1026–36

Penning, R., Muller, C. and Clomps, L. (1969) Mortalité et causes de décès des épileptiques', *Psychiatria Clinica (Basel), 2*, 85–94

Prudhomme, C. (1941) 'Epilepsy and suicide', *Journal of Nervous and Mental Disease, 94*, 722–31

Purchase, W.B. and Wollaston, H.W. (1957) *Jervis on Coroners*, 9th edn, Sweet & Maxwell, London

Robins, E., Murphy, G.E., Wilkinson, R.H., Gassner, S. and Kayes, J. (1959) 'Some Clinical Considerations in the Prevention of Suicide based on a Study of 134 Successful Suicides', *American Journal of Public Health, 49*, 888–98

Sainsbury, P. (1955) *Suicide in London*, Chapman & Hall, London

—— (1971) 'Medical Research Council Clinical Psychiatry Unit', *Psychological Medicine, 1*, 429–36

—— (1983) 'Validity and Reliability of Trends in Suicide Statistics', *World Health Statistics Quarterly, 36*, 339–48

Sainsbury, P. and Barraclough, B.M. (1968) 'Differences between Suicide Rates', *Nature, 220*, 1252

Schneider, K.O. (1950) *Psychopathic Personalities*, Deuticke, Vienna

Seager, G.P. and Flood, R.A. (1965) 'Suicide in Bristol', *British Journal of Psychiatry, 111*, 919–32

Serin, S. (1926) 'Une enquête medico-psychologique sur le suicide à Paris', *La Presse Medicale, November*, pp. 1404–6

Shepherd, D.M. and Barraclough, B.M. (1974) 'The Aftermath of Suicide', *British Medical Journal, 2*, 600–3

—— (1976) 'The Aftermath of Parental Suicide for Children', *British Journal of Psychiatry, 129*, 267–76

—— (1978) 'Suicide Reporting: information or entertainment?', *British Journal of Psychiatry, 132*, 283–7

—— (1979) 'Help for Those Bereaved by Suicide', *British Journal of Social Work, 9*, 69–74

—— (1980) 'Work and Suicide: an empirical investigation', *British Journal of Psychiatry, 136*: 469–78

Shneidman, E. and Farberow, N. (1961) *The Cry for Help*, McGraw-Hill, New York, p. 34

Sillanpaa, M. (1973) 'Medico-social Prognosis of Children with Epilepsy. Epidemiological study and analysis of 245 patients', *Acta Paediatrica Scandinavica, Supplement 96*

—— (1983) 'Social Functioning and Seizure States of Young Adults with Onset of Epilepsy in Childhood', *Acta Neurologica Scandinavica, Supplement 237*

Society of Actuaries (1954) *Impairment Study 1951*, Society of Actuaries, New York

Stengel, E. (1963) *Suicide and Attempted Suicide*, Penguin, London

Stepien, L., Bidzinski, J. and Mazurowksi, W. (1969) 'The Results of Surgical Treatment of Temporal Lobe Epilepsy', *Polish Medical Journal, 8*, 1184–90

Taylor, D.C. and Marsh, S.M. (1977) 'Implications of long-term follow-up studies in epilepsy: with a note on the cause of death' in Penry, J.K. (ed.), *Epilepsy: the 8th International Symposium*, Raven Press, New York, pp. 27–34

Thurston, G. (1976) *Coronership*, Barry Rose, Chichester

White, S.J., McLean, A.E.M. and Howland, C. (1979) 'Anticonvulsant Drugs and Cancer. (A cohort study in patients with severe epilepsy)', *Lancet, 2*, 458–61

Whitlock, F.A. (1986) 'Suicide and physical illness' in Roy, A. (ed.), *Suicide*, Williams & Wilkins, Baltimore

Zielinski, J.J. (1974) 'Epilepsy and Mortality Rate and Cause of Death', *Epilepsia, 15*, 191–201

Zilboorg, G. (1937) 'Considerations on Suicide', *American Journal of Orthopsychiatry, 7*, 15–31

Index